Understanding ourselves through the Torah

Our Purpose· Our Nature· Our Development

Contents

PART 1

OUR PURPOSE IN THE WORLD

HOW DO WE DEFINE SUCCESS IN

LIFE?

CHAPTER 1 - EVERY PERSON HAS A MEANINGFUL AND VALUABLE PURPOSE IN LIFE

"What do I want from life?" and, "What do I want to do with my life?" are two of the most important questions we ask ourselves.

These questions arise from a natural desire for meaning, value, purpose, significance, and success which is built into the human psyche. This desire comes from an inner recognition that we all have a spiritual purpose in this life. The accomplishment of that purpose will result in a spiritually successful and rewarding life. Everyone, regardless of their upbringing, social status, intelligence, financial situation, or any other external factor in life, can achieve the greatest spiritual success in life- G-d is the ultimate equal opportunity employer.

When we appreciate that our lives have a greater purpose beyond getting and spending, when we recognize the importance, meaning, value, and significance of our purpose in this world, we will be motivated to work towards the fulfillment of our purpose.

However, if someone isn't aware that his life has a spiritual purpose, he will miss out on the true opportunities he was created for. When someone doesn't discover his true purpose, he will often attempt to find some other purpose for his life. Unfortunately, whatever he finds, since it is not his true purpose, even if he achieves what he sets out to do, he will not in the end find spiritual, or deeper success in his life. Instead, he can only (possibly) achieve that thing which he sought.

It would seem to be very helpful and important for us to look into

**our lives to discover that our purpose is for something more than
the comforts and pleasures of this world.**

Dovid Hamelech (תהילים צ' י') taught us that "The days of our lives
are seventy years, and if we live a long life it is eighty years, and the
best of those days are filled with hard work and complications.
Rashi explains that even when a person achieves what would seem
to be the greatest achievements in this world- power, prestige,
health, wealth, love, power, etc., it's still not that good; even a
charmed life is short and the benefits are limited.

The *Ramchal* in the first chapter of the *Mesilas Yesharim* writes: not
one person in a thousand lives a life of predominant pleasure and
peace; and even would such a person to live, and live a hundred
years, his time would pass and the he would be gone as if he never
were.

The *Ramchal* tells us that this reality shows us that *Hashem* did not
create us for the purposes of pleasure and comfort. Therefore,
there must be a different purpose for our creation.

The *Mesilas Yesharim* explains that we have a *neshama* which is the
most important and special creation in the universe, and it is for the
purpose of that *neshama* that we were created. And so we must ask
ourselves- what is the purpose of our *neshama*? Why did *Hashem*
give us a *neshama*? What does He want us to do with it? Our
existence in this world seems to be so mundane and irrelevant.
Why do we need such an important *neshama*? Certainly, there
must be an important purpose to our lives.

**That *Hashem* created us with a *neshama* prompts within us a
motivation and an obligation to figure out and understand What
He wants and expects us to do with it.**

We spend most of our lives working hard; from school to work, to our endless to-do lists. We have painful experiences, health problems, difficulties in our important relationships, financial struggles, we lose people who are important to us; our lives are a constant barrage of struggle, anxiety, and frustration.

A thinking person will naturally contemplate the nature of his existence and the purpose of his life, but during difficult times the question, "What is the meaning of all this?" confronts us with great urgency.

There are a few basic questions that perennially circulate the periphery of our consciousness: "Why am I here? Is my life important? If so, in what way? Do I have value and significance in my life? Is my life worthwhile?"

These questions are all related to our understanding of our purpose in life. The answers to these questions are important and they are relevant in our lives on a constant basis. Even if we have the answers to these questions, which many of us do, or we are at least capable of saying the *right* words, it's helpful to clarify the concepts, to remind ourselves about them, and to focus on internalizing them and integrating them into our lives.

It's important to clarify Our Purpose in Life and Our Mission in Life. We also need to understand what brings Value and Significance to our lives, and to have an accurate definition of a Successful Life.

Chapter 2 - The Benefits Of Understanding Our Lives' Purpose

In a very general sense we are taught that our lives' purpose is not only to experience pleasure and comfort, rather, we are here to follow the ideals and values of *Hashem*. However, it's helpful to understand our purpose in a broader context.

There are a number of benefits that we receive from understanding that our lives' purpose is related to following the ideals and the values of *Hashem*. It will cause us to lead our lives in a manner that is truly productive. We will lead our lives in a way that will lead us to being able to receive the true benefits that *Hashem* will give us. We will also be much happier and more fulfilled both consciously and subconsciously.

We can only be successful in life when we are fulfilling our true purpose in this world. When we are not fulfilling our ultimate purpose in this world but rather spending our energies in the pursuit of other things, then our accomplishments are not really very important.

Most people have a powerful desire to achieve success in life in an over-arching sense. We want to be successful and we want to feel successful. However, when a person achieves success in a particular task or area, for example professional success, it will not, and we see every day in the world that it does not, by itself, result in transcendent feeling of a successful life. We see many people dedicate their lives to achieving a specific goal, and when they achieve it they discover, tragically, that it was all beside the point.

When we are not fulfilling our ultimate purpose but rather we are pursuing other interests, not only are we not achieving real success, we will also be plagued by (possibly subconscious) feelings of confusion, discontent, and unrest. This is because our lives, whether we realize it or not, have a specific purpose, and that purpose is not to be professionally successful (or wealthy or famous or powerful etc.). We all have a sense that true success is closely associated with meaning and real value. Therefore, the only way that we can genuinely feel successful is when we are leading a life that has meaning and real value in it. When we are fulfilling our true purpose in this world, even if we are lacking many popular definitions of a successful life, our lives become meaningful, valuable, gratifying, and satisfying.

The Importance of Clarifying the Specifics of Our Purpose:

Understanding the overall mission that we have, and dedicating our lives to living by it, is very helpful. Even when we know that success comes from serving *Hashem*, understanding this purpose of life with clarity can make the difference between achieving this success and living a successful life and missing the target and living a less successful life. Therefore, it is important for us to understand the specifics of our mission as well.

When we have an accurate understanding of the specifics of our mission, then we will pursue the proper projects. Those are the ones that have true meaning and value. Our lives will be more productive when we are doing more of that which is really important. We will also be receiving more of the benefits from *Hashem* when we are pursuing the projects that *Hashem* really wants us to be pursuing.

Leading our lives in a way that we are fulfilling our purpose, and we are doing our mission is really a truly successful life. The extent that we are able to live up to these goals is the way to measure our success in our lives.

The benefits of having an accurate definition of success is in three areas. It helps us to figure out what the proper projects are (those that have true meaning and value), it helps us to figure out what the proper process of growth is, and it helps us to have the proper method to asses ourselves and others (our assessments are very much related to our definitions of success).

Therefore, in order to figure out how to be truly successful in life we need to figure out what our purpose is, what is really valuable, and what is really meaningful.

CHAPTER 3 - WHY DID HASHEM CREATE THE WORLD?

Comprehending what *Hashem* had in mind when He created the world is not a simple task. Therefore, it's difficult to define and understand our purpose in life, and it is especially difficult to apply that knowledge in a practical sense. However, we need to do our best to understand it and to apply it:

Understanding our purpose begins with a fundamental question – How did we get here? A different way to phrase this is – Where did humans begin? Understanding that we didn't come into existence by chance, rather, *Hashem* created us intentionally, and for a reason is the first step in the understanding of our purpose.

The understanding that *Hashem* created the world intentionally, and for a reason is also an important step in understanding our purpose.

Another matter that is very relevant to our understanding of our purpose and our mission relates to the fact that *Hashem* gave the *Torah* to us and He instructed us to study the *Torah* and to keep its laws.

<u>דרך ה' - פרק ב</u>
הבריאה בעיקרית... היא במין האנושי, וכל שאר הנבראים... בעבורו
להשלמת ענינו.

<u>אור הצפון - ספר תולדות אדם</u>
השי"ת ברא בשביל (אדם) את הבריאה כולה.

The most important creation of *Hashem* is Man. The rest of the universe, plants, animals, sky, mountains, stars, etc. was created to assist a person in accomplishing his goals. Putting these ideas together, we understand that the reason and purpose that *Hashem* created the world was for the purpose of Man and for Man's purpose.

More specifically, the very first words of the תורה tell us, according to רש"י, that *Hashem's* goal in creating the world was for the purpose of כלל ישראל:

בראשית ברא אלוקים –for "ראשית" the Jewish nation, *Hashem* created the world

The גמרא סנהדרין לז tells us that every person can say about himself בשבילי נברא העולם!

Hashem created the entire world for the purpose of each person individually! Our purpose in life can be described as To Serve *Hashem*/Keep the *Torah* in This World.

Another way this can principle can be expressed is like this:

● *Hashem* created אדם and חוה as exalted beings with an exalted purpose.

● The entire world was created by *Hashem* as a vehicle for them and their offspring to fulfill this purpose.

● *Hashem* gave us the תורה to guide us in how to fulfill this purpose.

Another matter that plays a big role in understanding what our purpose is relates to the nature of a human being. We are not just like all of the animals, we are not merely intelligent apes. Our existence is not limited to this world. The Torah tells us that every person was created in the "Image of *Hashem*"! We all have very important responsibilities in this world, and we have an eternal existence where we will be able to have an eternal relationship with the creator of the world. All of these factors give us some of the context of who we are and what our purpose in this world is.

CHAPTER 4 - WHY DID HASHEM CREATE US?

Let's examine these points individually in greater depth:

The next step in defining our purpose in the world and our mission in life is to clarify why *Hashem* created the world and why *Hashem* created people. Understanding *Hashem's* reason for creating us defines our lives' purpose. Understanding the reason that *Hashem* had for creating us also helps us to understand what our mission is, what will bring us true value and significance in life, and what an accurate definition of true success is. Therefore, it is important to clarify the answer to this question!

<u>*Hashem* created the world for the purpose of doing חסד – Giving.</u>

<u>דרך ה' - פרק ב</u>
התכלית בבריאה היה להטיב... לזולתו.

Hashem created the world in order to benefit others; meaning, not for His own needs or benefit

<u>דרך ה'- פרק ב</u>
כוונתו יתברך שמו בבריאה שברא, לברוא מי שיהיה נהנה בטובו יתברך באותו הדרך שאפשר שיבנה בו.

Hashem created the entire world for the purpose of giving, doing חסד to people. And so ה' created the person and the world to facilitate this purpose in the best possible way.

Now that we know why the world was created for us, (for us to have ultimate good) we must ask how we can best accomplish this purpose.

מסילת ישרים - פרק א
האדם לא נברא אלא להתענג על ה', וליהנות מזיו שכינתו, שזהו התענוג
האמיתי... ומקום העדון הזה באמת הוא העולם הבא... אך הדרך כדי להגיע
אל מחוז חפצינו זה הוא זה העולם.

The מסילת ישרים explains that *Hashem* created us to have ultimate good, ultimate benefit, in the World to Come. However, *Hashem* created a system where a person must earn this ultimate good. We must first live in this world and lead a life following the values and guidelines of the *Torah*. Then we can receive the ultimate benefit in the World to Come.

To summarize, our purpose in life is: *to receive ultimate benefit in the World to Come*. However, it can also be described as a mission: *to do the מצות/follow the values and guidelines of the Torah in This World.*

Our Purpose - Our Mission

There are different ways to describe our mission in the world:

אור הצפון - מדת החסד - ערכו של חסד
תכלית בריאת האדם היא שילך בדרכיו של הקב"ה... והלכת בדרכיו... מה
הוא רחום אף אתה רחום
חסד, זהו תפקידו הרם, ורק ע"י מילואו בכחו להתעלות למדרגה הנישאה...
מה הוא רחום ,מהו התפקיד להדמות לקונו
חסד הוא העיקר, השורש. ממנו יניקתו, קיומו וגידולו של האדם, וכל המעשה
שהאדם עושה הם ענפים

The אור הצפון explains that our overall mission in life is to emulate the ways of *Hashem* and to develop ourselves to have the character traits of *Hashem* - מה הוא רחום אף אתה רחום. The *Alter* explains that all the different מצות and expectations that we have all revolve around this general theme.

מסילת ישרים - הקדמה
השלימות האמיתי הוא רק הדביקות בו יתברך... ואני קרבת אלוקים לי טוב

ראוי לו שתהיה כל פנייתו רק לבורא יתברך ושלא יהיה לו שום תכלית אחר בכל מעשה שיעשה... אלא להתקרב אליו יתברך ולשבור כל המחיצות המפסיקות בינו לבין קונו

The מסילת ישרים explains that our mission is to achieve an attachment and closeness (דביקות) to *Hashem*. Everything we do in life can affect this closeness, either it can bring us closer to *Hashem*, or it can pull us away from *Hashem*.

The מסילת ישרים specifies general categories, such as having the qualities of יראת השם, אהבת השם, טהרת הלב, ללכת בכל דרכיו, and to follow all of the מצות and guidelines that *Hashem* gives us in the *Torah*.

The מ"י explains each of these different areas.

יראת ה refers to יראת הרוממות, which refers to being in awe of *Hashem*. This requires us to learn about *Hashem*, to understand *Hashem's* greatness, and to be inspired and motivated to be like *Hashem*.

ללכת בכל דרכיו means to follow in all of *Hashem's* ways. This works well with the first step of developing an awe (respect/admiration) of *Hashem*. Once we can understand *Hashem* better and we can respect and admire who *Hashem* is and what *Hashem* does, then we can genuinely be inspired to want to follow in the ways of *Hashem*.

אהבת השם refers to feelings of love for *Hashem* that include a desire for His will to be done both by ourselves and others.

טהרת הלב refers to a person's motivation for his actions to be coming from the proper places. This also includes a person focusing his thoughts and feelings at the moment as opposed to acting robotically.

There are many details that are included in the guidelines of the

Torah. The entire שׁוּלְחָן עָרוּךְ together with all of the סִפְרֵי הֲלָכָה teach us the עֲבוֹדָה שֶׁבַּגּוּף, the external tasks we must do to serve ה'. There is also עֲבוֹדָה שֶׁבַּלֵּב, internal tasks, מִדּוֹת and טָהֳרַת הַלֵּב that we need to develop.

The מְסִלַּת יְשָׁרִים tells us – זְהִירוּת-זְרִיזוּת-נְקִיּוּת-פְּרִישׁוּת-טָהֳרָה, וכו' – this is the method to achieve the goal.

Since our mission in life is to "Live by the values and rules of the *Torah*", success (in life) corresponds to how much we are trying to live by the values and the rules of the *Torah*.

CHAPTER 5 - WHY DID HASHEM GIVE US THE TORAH AND THE MITZVOS?

 The translation of "*Mitzvos*" is "commandments". However, the context of these *mitzvos*/commandments is unclear. There are many situations where authority figures create rules and expectations. It can be from a government, an employer, a teacher, or a parent. The rules and expectations can be created for a number of reasons. At times, the authority figure has their own needs that they are enforcing, at times, there are community needs that are being enforced, and at times, it is for the benefit of the person who is being asked to listen. When *Hashem* gives us the *mitzvos*, what is *Hashem's* motivation?

<u>ספר חפץ חיים - הקדמה</u>
ברוך ה' אלקי ישראל אשר הבדילנו מכל העמים, ונתן לנו תורתו... כדי שנזכה לקיים כל מצותיו. וכל כוונתו הוא רק לטובותינו.

As we have shown, *Hashem's* entire purpose for creating the world was for חסד - to give people an opportunity to serve *Hashem* and earn reward. Similarly, the חפץ חיים writes, the תורה and the מצות were created and given to us in the same way — so that through them we may earn *Hashem's* greatest reward.

<u>וואיטער בהקדמה</u>
כתוב (במדבר טו') "למען תזכרו ועשיתם את כל מצותי, והייתם קדושים לאלוקיכם." ויהיה ביכלתינו לקבל את השפעת טובו ורב חסדו בעולם הזה ובעולם הבא, כמו שכתוב (דברים י') "מה ה' אלוקיך שואל מעמך, כי אם... לשמור את מצות ה' ואת חקותיו אשר אנכי מצוך היום לטוב לך." ועיין שם בפרוש הרמב"ן דהאי "לטוב לך" אתחלת הפסוק ד"מה ה' אלקך שאל מעמך" קאי.

The חפץ חיים writes that we see from these פסוקים the reason

Hashem gave us the תורה and the מצות is so that we can become "קדוש" and experience that greatest reward. Hashem didn't give us the Torah and the mitzvos for any other reason. Hashem doesn't need us to serve Him for His benefit.

The recognition that the responsibility to follow the Torah and the mitzvos is for our benefit can give us extra motivation to be committed to keeping the laws properly.

CHAPTER 6 - IN WHAT WAY DID HASHEM DESIGN US?

Hashem created us incomplete. Our goal and responsibility is to follow the *Torah's* מצות to make ourselves better.

This axiom leads us to the following questions:

What is the intrinsic nature of a human being?

Why was it important for *Hashem* to have designed a human being in an imperfect fashion?

How does the specific design of a human being help us fulfill our purpose in the world in the best way possible?

Different Parts of a Human Being – (*Hashem* designed a human being with different parts.)

<u>תורת אברהם - קצב'</u>
מורכב הוא משני עולמות, שמים וארץ השתתפו, נשמת חיים ועפר מן האדמה.

<u>אור הצפון – האדם והבחירה ריד'</u>
מורכב מחלק שכלי ומחלק בהמי.
חלק בהמי – אין לפניו אלא תאוותו והנאתו הרגעית, ללא כל מחשבה והבחנה.
חלק שכלי – חושב מחשבות, בוחן כל דבר בחשבון ודעת, ויודע להשכיל בחכמה ודעת.

On one hand, a person has amazing parts to him – a person has a נשמה and a שכל.

A person also has a physical nature.

The נשמה and שכל can lead a person toward greatness, but the גוף can lead a person away from greatness.

אבות - פרק ג
חביב אדם שנברא בצלם... שנאמר בצלם אלוקים עשה את האדם.

אור הצפון - צלם אלוקים
נשתדל להשתלם להיות האדם כצורתו האמיתי... להנהיג על פי ההתדמות
אליו... ("זה אלי ואנוהו" – הוי דומה לו, מה הוא רחום אף אתה – הכוללת בו
כל... ההשתלמות על ידי ההתדמות לו.)

The greatness of humanity can be described as - *the nature and capacity to act with all of the great attributes /* מדות *of Hashem.* *Hashem* acts with and personifies His great מדות. Humans, in our own way, have the capacity to attain all of these מדות of *Hashem*. When we make ourselves G-dly in this way, we realize the ultimate potential of our existence. This highest level of human accomplishment is described by the מסילת ישרים as "שלימות" – "Wholeness" or "Completeness" and "דביקות בה"" – being "Close", literally "Attached" to *Hashem*.

However, only part of our design seems to help us with our mission.

Our נשמה helps us fulfill our purpose and our mission in this world, but our חלק בהמי, our physical nature, works against our purpose and our mission:

אור הצפון - האדם והבחירה
מציאות האדם מורכב הוא מחלק שכלי ומחלק בהמי. ההבדל בין שני
החלקים רב מאד. והם ניגודים זה לזה.
חלק בהמי אין לפניו אלא תאוותו והנאתו הרגעית ללא כל מחשבה והבחנה.

תורת אברהם - קצב'
דו פרצופים שלו את גדלו ויכלתו עד התדמות אל השם ואת קטנו ושפלותו

Our physical nature is described as a lowly part of a person. This חלק הבהמי, this physical nature, causes a person to follow the impulses of his physical desires instead of serving *Hashem*.

מסילת ישרים - הקדמה
שמו הקב"ה לאדם במקום שרבים בו המרחיקים אותו ממנו יתברך והם הם
התאוות החומריות אשר אם נמשך אחריהן הנה הוא מתרחק והולך מן הטוב
האמתי.

מסילת ישרים - פרק יג
אין לך תענוג עולמי אשר לא ימשוך אחריו איזה חטא בעקבו

We have a very important mission in life which is related to our
נשמה and our שכל, but our גוף and our physical desires pull us away
from fulfilling our true goals and mission.

The מסילת ישרים in the הקדמה describes some of the goals of עבודת
השם: developing an awe of *Hashem*, following in the ways of
Hashem, developing character traits, having sincerity of heart,
doing all the מצות.

The מסילת ישרים explains the process of internal development. Each
level of growth relates to a person developing a greater genuine
commitment to *Hashem* and the מצות while simultaneously
becoming less attached to physical needs and desires. Many of the
stages of spiritual development are directly related to a person
being less involved in the physical world, such as קדושה, טהרה, פרישות,
יחוד המעשה.

Why Did *Hashem* Create Us the Way He Created Us?

Despite the fact that our physical nature causes us to be drawn
towards self-destructive things and away from spiritual things, we
cannot live without satisfying our physical needs.

Why did *Hashem* create Man with a חלק הבהמי, with a compulsion to
act against the *Torah* and to do things that are harmful to
ourselves? Why weren't we created with only the נשמה and the שכל
which draw us naturally to what is good for us? Would that not be a

better חסד from *Hashem* toward a human being?

If we compare the way *Hashem* created a person to the way *Hashem* created a מלאך, the מלאך seems better off. מלאכים live in a world without תאווה and without עבירה; consequently, without cancer and war and heartache and death. We know that *Hashem's* greatest חסד was toward Man, we just need to understand how and why.

אור הצפון - האדם והבחירה

מלאכים... אין להם בחירה, הם רואים לפניהם את גודל קדושתו של הקב"ה, ובהכרח מקיימים את רצונו.

A מלאך seems to have the perfect makeup. A מלאך will always do the רצון ה'. There is nothing in its nature that pulls it away from ה', therefore a מלאך will always be דומה to ה'. On the other hand, a human is created with strong needs and desires for the pleasures of the world. The drive for these needs and desires is so strong that it's almost impossible not to do the wrong thing in some form at some time, as חז"ל tell us - אין אדם צדיק בארץ אשר יעשה טוב ולא יחטא. Furthermore, if we were ultimately created for the eternal ecstasy of עולם הבא why didn't *Hashem* just put us there directly? Why did He create this world for the doing of מצות and עבירות at all?

These questions lead us to recognize that our mission is more complicated than just "Live by the values and the rules of the Torah" (because if that was our whole mission, then *Hashem* would have designed us in a way that we would naturally follow all the רצון ה'). This indicates that there must be other aspects to our mission! It also means that there are other elements that construct what is truly valuable and meaningful, and therefore define what is ultimate success!

CHAPTER 7 - WE NEED TO OVERCOME CHALLENGES FOR REAL ACCOMPLISHMENT. CHALLENGES ARE OPPORTUNITIES FOR GROWTH.

מסילת ישרים - פרק א

והנה, שמו הקב"ה לאדם במקום שרבים בו המרחיקים אתו ממנו יתברך, והם הם התאוות החומריות, אשר אם נמשך אחריהן, הנה הוא מתרחק והולך מן הטוב האמתי.

עולם הזה is filled with obstacles that hamper us from our true purpose of being close to *Hashem*. In other words, the nature of man and the nature of the world interact in a way that inherently and intrinsically create challenges for a person to be able to serve *Hashem* properly.

עיקר מציאות האדם בעולם הזה הוא רק לקיים המצות, ולעבוד ולעמוד בניסיון.
כפי השיעור אשר כבש את יצרו ותאוותיו ונתרחק מן המרחיקים אותו מן הטוב ונשתדל לדבק בו, כן ישיגהו וישמח בו.

The מסילת ישרים explains that the only true accomplishment in this world comes through doing מצות and overcoming challenges; accordingly, true or ultimate good for a person can only come from this true accomplishment.

Therefore, *Hashem's* greatest חסד to a human being is to create the world in a way that it constantly challenges a person to do the proper thing. Through a person overcoming his challenges he can receive the greatest benefits and rewards that *Hashem* created. This is the reason why *Hashem* created Man with a nature that draws us towards physical needs, and why *Hashem* created a world for us that naturally pulls us away from being able to serve Him properly.

♦ The דרך ה' spells out these steps:

דרך ה' – פרק ב

כוונתו יתברך שמו... לברוא מי שנהנה בטובו יתברך.
להיות בטוב שלם... ראוי שיהיה... מי שיקנה בטוב בעצמו.
על כן גזר וסידר שיברא עניני שלימות ועניני חסרון, ותברא בריה שיהיה בה
אפשריות לשני העניינים... ויותנו לבריה אמצעים שעל ידם תקנה לעצמה את
השלימות.
היא תקרא עיקרית שבכל הבריאה, וכל שאר מה שימצא במציאות לא יהיה
אלא עוזר... הבריאה העיקרית... המין האנושי.

1. 'ה created the world for Man's good.

2. True Good is only achieved by overcoming challenges towards spiritual growth.

3. The entire world was created to promote this master plan.

A person has constant opportunities to do good things, but his nature, and the nature of the world, are designed to challenge him in the doing of good. However, 'ה creates us with the ability to overcome the challenges. **This is the עיקר, the main reason, 'ה created the world.**

Challenges Are Opportunities for Choices

אור הצפון - האדם והבחירה

כאן היא גדולתו של האדם, המלאכים הם בבחינה "עומדים" שאין להם
בחירה... מה שאין כן באדם. ה' ברא את האדם בצלם דמות תבניתו, וכשם
שהוא רבון העולמים, והיינו לפעול ולעשות בכל העולמות כרצונו, כן הטביע כח
באדם לקבוע את דרכו על הארץ ולבחור בחיים או במות, בטוב או ברע, ובזה
עולה גדולתו וקדושתו על המלאכים.

The אור הצפון explains that even though in certain ways a מלאך is greater than a person, a מלאך can't "Choose to do good." It is a

מלאָך's nature to do good; there isn't any challenge that the מלאָך is overcoming when he serves *Hashem*.

If "True Greatness" and "True Accomplishment" were determined based upon the results of whether the right thing was always done or not, then an angel would be greater than a human. The challenges which face a person, and overcoming them, are what make us the greatest of *Hashem's* creations; greater even than the מלאכים whose very essence is קדושה and רוחניות.

We see this concept in the Torah in an exchange between יעקב and יצחק. *Chazal* tell us that at the end of יצחק's life his יצר הרע had left him completely. His תאוות were completely defeated and the only desire that remained for יצחק was a desire for רוחניות and closeness to ה'. At that point, יצחק's nature was such that it wasn't a challenge for him to do מצות and not to do עבירות. His nature was similar to a מלאָך – a being whose entire nature is to serve *Hashem*. (ויצא כח' יג' רש"י ד"ה ואלוקי)

However, when יעקב described the state of יצחק at the time, he was hesitant to refer to the fact that יצחק was like a מלאָך, that his father had no more temptation to do anything wrong. (A slight departure in perspective that some people have about what true greatness looks like.) יעקב felt that it would be a lack of respect to יצחק to refer to the fact that יצחק's state was such that he didn't have any more challenges.

The ספר דברי דוד explains that רש"י means that when a person is in this world and he has challenges that he needs to overcome, that is a more exalted state than being in a situation where there aren't any challenges to overcome.

The recognition that "Having challenges is necessary for real accomplishment" clarifies to us that our mission in life is not merely to live by the values and the rules of the *Torah*. Rather, it is to overcome challenges in order to live by the values and the rules

of the *Torah*. This also helps us redefine what is really valuable and meaningful in life, and it also gives us a different understanding of real success. Real success is our ability to overcome challenges to keep the *Torah*, not the technical keeping of the *Torah* in an objective vacuum.

There are many benefits to realizing that our mission in life is overcoming our challenges. One of the helpful perspectives is that it gives us a sense of meaning to the challenges that we have. Another is that we can feel the greatest sense of accomplishment when we know that we have striven our utmost even if the external result is not greatly noticeable to others.

CHAPTER 8 - WHY DID HASHEM GIVE US THE TORAH EVEN THOUGH WE MAY FAIL MANY OF OUR CHALLENGES?

As we wrote before, *Hashem* created Man with a compulsion to not keep the *mitzvos* in order to create the opportunity for us to grow by overcoming challenges. For this same reason, *Hashem* gave us the *Torah*, His greatest treasure, even though we are not capable of completely understanding or even following the *Torah*. Since *Hashem's* intention was to create a system wherein we have endless opportunities for growth, the *Torah's* ideal is something even the greatest person must continue to strive towards and work for.

The גמרא in שבת relates a discussion between משה רבינו, ה', and the מלאכים about whether the תורה is appropriate for Man.

שבת פח:

בשעה שעלה משה למרום אמרו מלאכי השרת לפני הקב"ה "מה לילוד אשה
בינינו?" אמר להן "לקבל תורה בא." אמרו לפניו, "חמודה גנוזה... אתה מבקש
ליתנה לבשר ודם?"

מכתב מאליהו – חלק ג' – גלות וגאולה

טענת המלאכים "מה אנוש כי תזכרנו" עניינה הוא שהמלאכים אין להם שום
מושג על מהות הבחירה, ולכן הבקורת שלהם על החטא חריפה מאד. מבקרים
הם גם את אפשרות 'הוא אמינא' לחטוא ועל כן הבקורת שלהם מתיחסת גם אל
הבוחר בטוב על שהיתה לו בכלל מלחמת הבחירה, שלרגע אחד נראה בעיניו
השקר לאמת.

מלאכים can see only the truth in the world. They understand and appreciate the greatness of *Hashem* and they are programmed to only serve *Hashem*. There is no way for מלאכים to do anything that would go against the 'רצון ה; they have no בחירה. The human ability to act against the 'רצון ה was viewed by the מלאכים as a חסרון and a reason that the תורה should not be given to בני ישראל.

The מהרש"א explains why the מלאכים felt the תורה should not be given to humans.

מהרש"א ד"ה מה אנוש כי תזכרנו וגו'

כי הם באים מילוד אשה ואינם מוכנים לקבל נסתר של התורה שהוא דבר
רוחני... (והמלאכים) כולו רוחני מוכן יותר להשיג דבר רוחני מבן אדם המוטבע
בחומר.

The מלאכים said to 'ה that the נסתרי התורה is not appropriate for humans. The נסתרי התורה is, by nature, a "דבר רוחני." The מלאכים thought that the only being fit to be given the תורה is a perfect being; a being without a חלק גשמי, a being that is not capable of חטא.

הקב"ה told משה to answer the מלאכים and משה was afraid. משה said to 'ה, "They have a good point. They are כולו רוחני. That would seem to make them more ראוי to be given the נסתרי התורה. 'ה told משה - "אחוז בכסא כבודי"- "Hold on to my כסא הכבוד." The מהרש"א explains this statement of 'ה to be in the same vein as the גמרא in שבת קנב: which says, "שנשמות הצדיקים צרורות בצרור החיים תחת כסא הכבוד" which means, simply, that we have the capacity to reach the כסא הכבוד if we follow the מצות and serve 'ה to the best of our ability; therefore, humanity is מוכן to receive the נסתרי התורה.

What comes out of this dialogue between משה and the מלאכים is that humanity's capacity for growth and spiritual self-determination makes us more ראוי for the תורה than the מלאכים. We cannot fully understand the תורה much less keep its laws perfectly, compared to the מלאכים who can only keep the תורה perfectly. But the תורה is ours because the realization of the תורה's purpose is growth and working to overcome challenges, not perfection.

In Summary:

1) *Hashem's* purpose for creating the world was to give people the opportunity to earn a share in the World to Come, a world of complete and perfect good.

2) The only way for us to earn our share in עולם הבא is to live a life of overcoming challenges to do *mitzvos* and serving *Hashem*.

3) Therefore, *Hashem* created people and *Hashem* created this world in a way that we will have the opportunity to do the most *mitzvos* and overcome the greatest challenges in their pursuit. Therefore, even though, from a certain point of view, a person's goal in life is to perfect his מדות such as הליכה בדרכיו [following all of the ways of *Hashem*], יושר המדות [developing the appropriate character traits], אהבת השם [the appreciation and love of *Hashem*], שמירת כל המצות [doing all of the commandments of *Hashem*], יראת השם [having an appreciation of *Hashem* and being in awe of *Hashem* and fearing *Hashem*], and to learn and know all the תורה, however, a person's mission in life is really to do his best to overcome his challenges in the process of striving towards these objectives.

CHAPTER 9 - MEASURING OUR ACCOMPLISHMENTS, OUR CHOICES ARE INFLUENCED BY MANY FACTORS

A person's thoughts, feelings, and behaviors are influenced by many different factors. Our nature, our environment, and our experiences all play a major role in affecting the way that we think, feel, and act.

אורחות צדיקים - הקדמה

כל הדעות-יש מהם דעות שהיו לאדם מתחילת ברייתו לפי טבע גופו, ויש מהם דעות שטבעו של אדם זה מכוון ועתיד לקבל אותם מהרה יותר משער הדעות, ויש מהם שאינם לאדם מתחילת ברייתו אלא למד אותם מאחרים, או שפונה להם מעצמו לפי מחשבה שעלתה בלבו, או ששמע שזאת הדעה טובה לו ובה ראוי לילך, והנהיג עצמו בה עד שנקבעה בלבו.

"Nature or Nurture" as origin for our behavior and personality is a topic of many discussions. Which one influences us more? The אורחות צדיקים is telling us that they both have a major influence on us.

He also explains that both of these factors influence us in every aspect of our lives:

יש אדם שהוא בעל חמה..גבה לב..בעל תאוה..מהולל ואונן, כילי ושוע, אכזרי ורחמן, רך לבב ואמיץ כח.

All of these מדות are influenced to a great extent by both our nature, our environment, and our experiences.

כל מדות האדם אשר תראה בהם בימי הבחרות והזקנה, הן היו בימי הילדות והשחרות... בימי הזקנה אינם נעתקים בקל ממה שהיו בו בימי הבחרות. והם

דומים לטס כסף שהיה טמון בקרקע והעלה חלודה עבה באורך הטמנתו, צריך
אותו כסף מריקה אחר מריקה עד שישוב הכסף למראהו הנאה.

The core nature that we are born with or that which we have
developed is mostly already developed by the time a person ıs a
young adult. That means that many of the main factors that
influence our thoughts, feelings, and behaviors are a part of us
without our adult decision for them to be there.

Our nature, our nurture and our environment affect us to such an
extent that there are some people who claim that there is no such
thing as "Free will." Our good choices are only the result of the
positive forces in our life, whether internal or external, which
compel us to behave appropriately. The bad choices in our life are
made by a similar non-voluntary process. This philosophy would
compare human decisions to the decisions of animals whose
behaviors are determined by instinctual reactions that compel them
to choose one way or the other. These people believe a person's
choices are merely a more sophisticated form of an animal's
decision-making process- an instinctual decision that is determined
by the forces in the person's psyche.

We Have the Ability to Choose

<u>רמב"ם פרק ה' הלכות תשובה</u>

רשות לכל אדם נתונה אם רצה להטות עצמו לדרך טובה ולהיות צדיק הרשות
בידו. ואם רצה להטות עצמו לדרך רעה ולהיות רשע הרשות בידו... ואין לו
מי שיכפהו ולא גוזר עליו. ודבר זה עיקר גדול הוא והוא עמוד התורה
והמצוה. אילו הא-ל היה גוזר על האדם להיות צדיק או רשע... ומה מקום היה
לכל התורה כולה?

There are many challenges that face us throughout the course of
our lives. Some are harder than others. Some seem to be nearly
impossible to overcome at times. As we have shown from many
מאמרי חז"ל in the previous chapters, our purpose in life and the
purpose for which *Hashem* created people and the world is for us to
choose good, to choose to do the right things in these difficult

moments and in these challenging areas. The רמב"ם comes to reassure us, to gainsay the "טיפשי אומה"ע" and even the "רוב גולמי בני ישראל," that our fate and our destiny to be either a צדיק or a רשע is pre-prescribed. The רמב"ם exhorts us to understand that we have the ability to choose good no matter how predetermined our path in life might seem to be. Otherwise, says the רמב"ם, how can there be reward and punishment? How can we have a *Torah* which instructs us what to do? It is because we do have the ability to choose good, to choose to serve 'ה in our lives.

♦ Though we have the ability to choose despite the forces that push and pull us in different directions, those forces do play a role in our level of responsibility and in determining the level of our accomplishment.

אור ישראל - אגרת ו

בכל פרט העבירה נבדלים בני אדם זה מזה בקבלת עונשם לפי תכונתם ומצבם... עשיר עני, חכם סכל, זריז ועצל בטבעו, וכיוצא הרבה והרבה בחינות שונות וכל אשר תקל לפני האדם להישמר מהעבירה כן תגדל עונשה.

All of these factors influence how easy or difficult it is for an individual to make the right decision in any given situation. The factors affect the degree of responsibility that we have to make the proper decision and the degree of accomplishment when we overcome a challenge.

When we have chosen to do the proper thing despite the situation being difficult, that indicates that we are really sincere about our service of *Hashem*, and that is a major accomplishment.

A Choice That Involves Sincerity Is A Real Accomplishment

עלי שור - דעת עצמינו

יש חילוק בין "הכרעה" ל"בחירה"

בלי דעת אין בחירה... תינוק מרגיש הנאה וצער, וגם יש לו רצון והוא גם עושה הכרעה. אבל הכרעתו הוא רק "אינסטינקט" ואין בו "שיקול שכלי". הרבה פעמים יש מאבק בן שני נגיעות, "שאיפה להנאה" כנגד "פחד בפני

העונש"... הנגיעה הגוברת בלבו היא המכריע.
להתגברותו של אינסטינקט אחד על משנהו אין לקרוא בשם בחירה...
טבעיים, חינוך, הרגל, נגיעות, כולם יכולים לפעול בגדר של הכרעה...וכולם
שולטים בנו כמעט שלטון מוחלט בחיינו.

There are different types of decisions that we make. Some decisions
that we make are truly a result of our free will. This is when the
decision is made with our שכל measuring whether it's a proper
decision or not. (The מכתב מאליהו explains בחירה in the following
way-The sense of responsibility to the truth which can be either
adopted or rejected based on a person's will). That is real בחירה.
However, when a decision is made without it coming from our שכל's
decision to do it, rather, it came from an instinct that overrode the
counter instincts, then that is not real בחירה. Rather, we were
merely compelled to this action based on the various forces in our
life at the time. This is not really בחירה. The different types of
matters that compel our decisions are matters such as our nature,
our training, our habits, and our desires. All of these elements
control us almost entirely. All of our thoughts, feelings, and
behaviors can be almost entirely controlled by these elements.
Therefore, often many of our decisions will end up merely being
compelled by these elements and our שכל is not actually measuring
and calculating our decisions. Our level of accomplishment is much
greater when we make the decision based upon our decision of our
שכל.

**Decision's that are made by our שכל are free will. Decisions that
are made due to compulsion are not coming from our free will.**

Sincerity Takes Place in Our Mind and Heart and It Isn't Always Reflected In Specific Actions

Shlomo Hamelech teaches us in *Mishlei* (ג ו) that "בכל דרכיך דעהו", "In
all of your ways you should know *Hashem*". The *Mesilas Yesharim*
(פרק טז) explains that this refers to the service of *Hashem* that is
related to our minds and hearts being focused on our dedication to

Hashem. He explains that " מי שיודע לטהר לבו יותר הוא המתקרב יותר והאהוב יותר אצלו יתברך". Our closeness to *Hashem* and that which *Hashem* appreciates is very much related to our thoughts and our heart. What we can see and measure are actions. Often, we will focus on doing the proper actions and we won't focus enough on developing the proper thoughts and feelings, because we give more value to our actions. We will also often measure success (either our own success or the success of others) based on actions more than based upon thoughts and feelings. This is either because we give more value to actions, or because it's easier to measure actions. However, the reality is that our thoughts and feelings are extremely valuable, and it's important to remember that when it comes to figuring out what our priorities are, and when it comes to evaluating ourselves or others.

When we are faced with a situation where there is a *mitzva* to be done, however, it is very difficult for us to do it. There may be a large financial investment that is necessary in order for us to do the *mitzva*, or, it may require a lot of physical or social discomfort in order to do the *mitzva*. In those situations, our dedication and sincerity are reflected in our actions. The *Torah* refers to these examples in the *Shema*. It says ואהבת את ה' אלוקיך בכל נפשך ובכל מאדך. This is telling us that doing the *mitzvos* even when it requires a real sacrifice; either of our money, or even our life, we must be dedicated enough to put the *mitzva* ahead of our money, or even our life. However, there are times when the *mitzva* itself can be completed without requiring much effort. Therefore, the fact that we did the *mitzva* doesn't reflect much sincerity. However, the level of our dedication to *Hashem* is an extremely important part of our *Avodas Hashem*, and that sincerity can be in our minds and hearts even when it's not reflected in our actions.

The *Zohar* is quoted as saying that "We are taught in the words of *Shema*, that we are responsible to give up our lives for the sake of *Hashem* in certain given situations."

If a person finds himself in that type of situation and he follows through and he gives up his life, that is certainly a major accomplishment. However, there is a means for us to accomplish that feat even in a situation where we are not currently having our lives threatened. If we sincerely think about what we would do in such a situation and we decide that we care about *Hashem's* commandments enough that we are ready to give up our lives if we would ever be in that situation. Then that is almost as good as if we had actually gone through with the experience". This is because the sincere decision that we are making is really the main part of our accomplishment.

תורת אברהם - מצות אנשים מלומדה

כל ערכה של המצוה נערך לפי מדת הרגשת עושיה.

The *Toras Avraham* explains that our thoughts and feelings are the most valuable (most important) part of the *mitzvos*. This should tell us that we should make it a high priority for ourselves to focus on having or developing the proper thoughts and feelings. Obviously, we need to do the *mitzvos* and we can't merely have the proper thoughts and feelings, however, we must prioritize both.

CHAPTER 10 - THE ABILITY TO OVERCOME OUR DIFFICULT CHALLENGES

It is essential for us to understand that we have the ability to overcome our challenges, and that we are not given challenges that are impossible to overcome. There are many factors in our lives that can often make it very difficult to make the proper decisions. If we don't think that we can overcome the challenges, then often we won't even try. It's likely that even if we do try, it won't be with the necessary amount of commitment to be able to succeed, because it's difficult to work hard on something that we don't think that it will be successful. However, even when it's clear to us that "free will" exists, and despite the fact that we have forces compelling us to make the wrong decisions, we can use our free will in order to make the proper decisions. It is still often difficult to recognize that we have free will to make the right decision even when the situation seems to be very difficult. An example of this is seen in the גמרא in סנהדרין.

סנהדרין קה
אמר להן נביא בישראל (ישעיה) חזרו בתשובה, אמרו לו אין אנו יכולים יצר הרע שולט בנו, (רש"י-אין אנו יכולים לייסר אותו)

The גמרא is telling us that even though the נביא was encouraging the people to overcome their challenges, and it seems that they may have even been motivated to try, however, they didn't think that they would be able to change. They thought that the challenges were too difficult for them to overcome. Therefore, they didn't make the proper attempt to change.

The truth is that in everyone's life there are consistently many challenges that we are faced with that really are too difficult for us to overcome based upon our own strength and wisdom alone. This is discussed in the גמרא in קידושין.

קידושין ל - יומא לח

אמר רבי שמעון בן לוי יצרו של אדם מתגבר עליו בכל יום ומבקש המיתו שנאמר צופה רשע לצדיק ומבקש המיתו, ואלמלא הקב"ה עוזרו לו אין יכול לו שנאמר אלוקים לא יעזבנו בידו (מהרש"א-הבא לטהר מסייעין אותו-יומא לח)

We are constantly faced with situations in life where we don't naturally have the strength, commitment, and wisdom to be able to do the right thing. However, *Hashem* set up the world in a fashion where this is often the case that *Hashem* will put us in a situation where we will not be able to do the proper thing based upon our own abilities, and we can only succeed together with the assistance from *Hashem*. Then, when we do show our sincerity and our genuine interest in succeeding, and we take the step to try to succeed, then *Hashem* gives us the help that we need in order to do what is right. Our job is to do the part of הבא לטהר, that we have to put in the effort, then it's up to *Hashem* to help us as much as *Hashem* sees fit.

מדרש איכה (ה-כא)

השיבנו השם אליך ונשובה-אמרה כנסת ישראל לפני הקב"ה רבונו של עולם שלך הוא (השיבנו) אמר להם שלכם הוא שנאמר שובה אלי ואשובה אליכם אמרה לפניו רבש"ע שלך הוא שנאמר שובינו אלקי ישעינו

עין יוסף

הכוונה דכנסת ישראל אומרת שלך היא-ר"ל שאתה תתחיל עמנו לעורר לבבנו לתשובה ואחר כך ונשובה אבל הקב"ה אומר שלכם היא-ר"ל שאתם צריכים להתחיל בתשובה ואז נעשה פשר דבר שישראל מתחילין כחודו של מחט השבה שלנו תלוי בך, שאין בנו כח ..והקב"ה פותח לבך כפתחה של אולם להתחיל אלא כחודו של מחט, ואתה תושיע לנו ותפתח לבבינו כפתחו של אולם

The מדרש seems to be relating to us what the reality is about what the nature is of the human struggle for positive change. Often people will have a sincere desire to change, however, they give up because it seems that change is too difficult. Or, at times, a person will not work hard himself, rather, he will look toward *Hashem* to solve the problem until *Hashem* weakens the challenge. This perspective is true, that it often is too difficult to difficult to change on our own. The מדרש gives us a guide for what we should do if we find ourselves in this situation. We shouldn't give up on our goal. We also shouldn't sit back and wait for *Hashem* to solve our problem for us. We shouldn't even wait for *Hashem* to make it easier before we start working on our own. Rather, we need to take the first big step; to show sincerity and determination to do what's right. Then *Hashem* will help us to accomplish our goals and to make it easier to overcome our challenges.

ברכות יז
רבון העולמים-גלוי וידוע לפניך שרצונינו לעשות רצוניך, ומי מעכב שעור
שבעיסה ושיעבוד מלכיות (רש"י-יצר הרע מהרש"א-מותר מביא להתגאות
ולתאוה; שיעבוד מלכיות מביא לידי תכלית השפלות
יהי רצון מלפניך שתצילנו מידם ונשוב לעשות חוקי רצוניך בלבב שלם

The גמרא is teaching us that the proper attitude that we should have (regarding the challenges that we have that seem to be too difficult). It is appropriate to have an attitude that I sincerely want to do what is right (the desire of *Hashem*), however, I am aware that there are both internal and external factors that make it difficult for me to always do the right thing. However, I really have the desire to do what is right (and that is the most important thing, to have the sincere desire to do what is proper). We also really want it to be easier for us to do the right thing. We communicate our feelings to *Hashem* (we tell *Hashem* that "I care"), and we ask *Hashem* to help. Then, we try our best to overcome our challenges. Once we know that we are capable of overcoming our challenges, and we know what the system that we need to use in order to get started, then, we can be motivated to work hard in order to do the right thing.

We Can Learn the Skills and Develop Our Character to Become More Skilled and More Capable to Overcome Our Challenges Over Time

Many of our challenges are very difficult for us to deal with because we are limited in our skills to deal with those challenges or because our character traits are not developed enough to deal with the situation in such a productive way. However, these things are able to be changed over time.

The תורת אברהם writes many chapters that relate to חכמת המוסר. One of the main lessons that he shares is that we have the ability to understand ourselves and to learn the skills of working on ourselves in order to help us overcome our challenges. We can learn to deal with the challenges productively when they are in front of us, we can learn to avoid putting ourselves in situations where we have significant challenges, and we can develop ourselves into the type of person who is less likely to have these נסיונות as much, or we can develop the strength to overcome our נסיונות even when they are significant.

CHAPTER 11 - REACHING SPIRITUAL HEIGHTS IS DESIGNED TO BE A PROCESS

אור הצפון - כח הירידה והעליה באדם
מדרש בראשית יז- אני נאה להקראות אדם ,שנבראתי מן האדמה.
אור הצפון - כל סוד מהותו ...מצד האחד גדול הוא מאד ונעלה מכל הברואים...
חכמתו מרובה משלכם. מהצד השני שכיון שנברא מן האדמה מוטל עליו ללכת
ולעלות ממדרגה למדרגה.

The *Alter* writes based on the *Midrash* that the two most fundamental aspects of being a Human Being are the fact that we have inherent greatness, and also that we need to develop that greatness in order to realize our incredible potential. We don't get to the מדרגה of being greater than the מלאכים without working to develop ourselves properly. A person is created in a way that he must "Climb the mountain" as opposed to being placed on top of the mountain.

Putting this idea together with the concepts of our previous chapters, we see that the reason *Hashem* created us to struggle for growth instead of saving us the trouble and simply placing us in a state of perfection is because in the eyes of *Hashem*, and therefore אפין אמת, climbing the mountain is being on top of the mountain.

רמב"ן בראשית כב' א'
ענין הנסיון הוא... להוציא הדבר מן הכח אל הפועל.

One of the reasons 'ה gives us challenges is because we grow specifically through challenging experiences.

The רמב"ן writes here that even אברהם אבינו, who was certainly on a very high מדרגה even before the עקדה, still needed to develop himself through experiences and challenges in life.

<u>ספר החינוך - מצוה ב' ברית מילה</u>

רצה להיות ההשלמה על ידי אדם ולא בראו שלם מבטן, לרמוז אליו כי כאשר
תשלום צורת גופו על ידו, כן בידו להשלים צורת נפשו, בהכשר פעולותיו.

The ספר החינוך explains that ברית מילה is a symbol and an archetype of *Hashem's* design for humanity. *Hashem* could have created us with the ברית מילה already done. Instead, right when we are born, *Hashem* shows us an example of what is to be the system for the rest of our lives: improving ourselves is a task that is given over to us.

<u>מסילת ישרים - הקדמה</u>

ראה שאין דברי החסידות ועניני היראה והאהבה וטהרת הלב דברים מוטבעים
באדם עד שלא יצטרכו אמצעים לקנותם, אלא ימצאו אותם בני אדם בעצמם
כמו שימצאו כל תנועותיהן הטבעיות, כשינה והיקיצה הרעב והשבע, וכל שאר
התנועות החקוקות בטבענו. אלא ודאי שצריכים הם לאמצעים ולתחבולות
לקנות אותם. ומסודר לפי ההדרגה המצטרכת בהם לקנות אותם על נכון. תורה
מביאה לידי זהירות, זהירות מביאה לידי זריזות... וכו'

The מסילת ישרים explains that the capacity for יראת ה' and אהבת ה' and טהרת הלב are inherent in our makeup like other natural human impulses such as sleeping and waking up. However, unlike sleeping and waking up, דברי חסידות must be consciously, intentionally developed. We don't need to be told that we need to sleep, to wake up, to eat, or to stop eating. We may need to adjust the amount of sleep that we get, or the amount of food that we eat, but the basic principles come to us naturally. However, people are not born with the proper thoughts, feelings, desires, and interests. Developing these spiritual *middos* requires time and effort to learn, to understand, and to cultivate.

The מסילת ישרים goes on to say that there are many aspects of spiritual development that can only be developed sequentially. The more basic levels of purity of character must be developed before other levels can be developed. The מסילת ישרים gives many examples of behaviors that would be appropriate for us if we were at a higher level of spiritual development. However, at an earlier point in the developmental process, those behaviors can be confusing and damaging to our spiritual journey.

One of the benefits of understanding that a major part of our mission relates to working to overcome the challenges that are in the way of our doing the *mitzvos* is that it gives us a positive picture of *Hashem's* relationship with us. Sometimes, when we face challenges in our lives, we may not have very positive feelings towards *Hashem*. But if we realize that a major part of our mission in this world is specifically to struggle in these situations, to overcome and grow from them, then we will have a different attitude about our challenges and about *Hashem* who gave us the challenges. It also can help us realize that the appropriate approach to spiritual growth is developing our greatness step by step.

רמב"ם - פירוש המשניות פרק חלק

אסור לאדם השלם שיאמר כשאעשה המצות שהם המדות הטובות ואתרחק מן העבירות שהם המדות הרעות שצוה השם יתברך שלא לעשותם, מה הוא הגמול שאקבל על זה, לפי שהוא כמו שיאמר הנער כשאני קורא זה מה יתנו לי, והם אומרים לו דבר פלוני. זהו מעלת אברהם שהוא עובד מאהבה.

The *Rambam* begins by telling us that the appropriate mentality that we should have when we are performing the *mitzvos* is that we want to do them because we appreciate their value, and we would do them even without any motivation that is related to reward and punishment.

ולפי שידעו חכמים שזה הענין קשה מאד ואין כל אדם משיג אותו, ואם השיגו אין מסכים בו בתחילת הענין.
האדם אינו עושה מעשה אלא כדי להגיע לו ממנו תועלת או שתסור ממנו פסידא, ואם אינו כן יהיה אצלו מעשה הבל וריק, היאך יאמר לבעל תורה עשה אלה המעשים, ולא תעשה אותם לא לירא מעונש ולא לקבל שכר, זה דבר קשה עד מאד, לפי שאין כל בני אדם משיגין האמת עד שיהיו כמו אברהם אבינו...לכן התירו להמון לעשות המצות לקבל שכר, ולהזהר מן העבירות מיראת העונש.

The *Rambam* explains that it is important for us to have realistic goals, and therefore, the rabbis have encouraged us to serve

Hashem at the level that we are up to. If we attempt to serve *Hashem* in a fashion that we are not ready for, it won't work.

בעשותם את המצות מיראת העונש ותקות הגמול..טוב להם עד שיהיה להם כח
ההרגל והשתדלות בעשיית התורה, ומזה יתעוררו לדעת האמת ויחזרו עובדים
מאהבה.. כמו שנתבאר פסחים דף נ' שמתוך שלא לשמה בא לשמה.

The *Rambam* explains that when we serve *Hashem* in a way that fits with where we are up to (what we are ready for), then through that process we will be able to reach a stage where we become ready for the next level of serving *Hashem*. This development is the appropriate and the productive way to do the *mitzvos*. It is similar to climbing a ladder or a mountain, which we need to ascend the mountain or the ladder one step at a time. Eventually, we will reach the top. However, if we attempt to go too quickly, we won't achieve anything that is meaningful or sustainable.

CHAPTER 12 - WE CAN'T EXPECT PERFECTION. WE ARE NOT BORN PERFECT. DEVELOPMENT TAKES TIME.

<u>מסילת ישרים - פרק ד</u>

עומק הדין עד היכן מגיע, אשר באמת ראוי להזדעזע ולהתחרד תמיד. כי מי
יעמוד ביום הדין ומי יצדק לפני בוראו באשר השקפתו מדקדקת על כל דבר קטן
או גדול... כך עולות בכף הקלות כמו החמורות... ולא יעלים הדיין עינו מהם
כלל... לא יניח מלשפוט ולהוכיח כל מעשה רע קטן כמות שהוא. ולהוציא מלב
הרוצים להתפתות ולחשוב שלא יעלה האדון ברוך הוא בדיניו הדברים הקלים
ולא יקח חשבון עליהם. אלא קללה הוא כל האומר הקב"ה ותרן יותרו מעוהי.
על הכל הוא דן ועל כל חטא הוא מעניש ואין להימלט.

Hashem has a system of justice that seems to be extremely strict. It
seems that any lack of perfection, even for what seems to be a
relatively small mistake is recognized by *Hashem*, and *Hashem*
holds us responsible for it, and *Hashem* punishes us for it. The fact
that *Hashem* holds us responsible means that we could have
avoided these mistakes and therefore, we are responsible for these
mistakes. This seems to mean that *Hashem* expects and demands
perfection from us, and we should also expect and demand
perfection from ourselves and from others.

אברהם הוא אברהם האהוב לקונו.. אברהם אוהבי, לא פלט מן הדין מפני דברים
קלים שלא דקדק בהם. על שאמר במה אדע אמר לו הקב"ה חייך ידוע תדע כי
גר יהיה זרעך וכו'.

Even the punishment that is given for any lack of perfection is very
significant. It seems that perfection is expected and demanded and
any lack of this perfection is punished in a severe way.

אורחות צדיקים - הקדמה

כל הדעות, יש מהם שהיו לאדם מתחילת ברייתו לפי טבע גופו, ויש מהן דעות שטבעו של אדם זה מכוון ועתיד לקבל אותם מהרה יותר משאר דעות, ויש שאינם לאדם בתחילת ברייתו אלא למד אותם מאחרים או שפונה לבו מעצמו לפי מחשבה שעלתה בלבו.

"גם במעלליו יתנכר נער, אם זך ואם ישר פעלו." (משלי כ, יא') מנעוריהם ניכר מדותיהם, כמו שתראה מקצת הנערים נראה בהם מדת הבשת, ומקצתם - העזות, ומקצתם נוטים אל התאווה, ומקצתם נוטים אל מעלות טובות. ודע כי כל מדות האדם אשר תראה בו בימי הבחרות והזקנות, הם היו בימי הילדות והשחרות, אך בזמן ההוא לא היה בו כח להראותם ולהביאם לידי המעשה. והנערים אשר גדלה עליהם נבלות, אפשר יוכל האדם להעתיקם אל הדרך הטובה, וכו' אבל בימי הזקנה אינם נעתקים בקל ממה שהיו בהם בימי הבחרות. והם דומין לטס כסף שהיה טמון בקרקע והעלה חלודה עבה באורך הטמנתו, צריך אותו הכסף מריקה אחר מריקה עד שישוב הכסף למראהו הנאה. כך האדם אשר הלך לפי דרכו ומנהגו ונשקע בעמקי המדות הגרועות, צריך ללטוש שכלו להבדיל בין הטמא ובין הטהור ולהרגיל בעבודה עד שיהיו המדות טבועות וקשורות בלבו.

The אורחות צדיקים explains that our character traits and tendencies come from various sources. Some come from our inborn nature and some are from our experiences, (especially from experiences that we have in early childhood). He also explains that when someone has a specific *middah* either from nature or nurture, it is very difficult to change. Generally, the same positive or negative character traits that we have when we are young, we have when we are old. This would seem to indicate that whatever negative character traits a person has will likely remain with him throughout his life. Even if he tries to work on changing himself it's likely that he will not be able to change his nature very much.

The מסילת ישרים we quoted in the previous chapter explained that the development of many of the ideal מדות, perspectives, and feelings take a very long time to develop. This tells us that it's expected that there will be many imperfections along the way toward spiritual perfection.

We consistently have an endless amount of responsibilities, yet we have powerful desires that are pulling us away from doing everything right, and our development in many areas of *Avodas Hashem* takes a long time. This creates a reality that "אֵין אָדָם צַדִּיק בָּאָרֶץ אֲשֶׁר יַעֲשֶׂה טוֹב וְלֹא יֶחֱטָא"; that it's virtually impossible to not do anything wrong. The reality seems to be that even when a person works really hard in order to do the right thing, he will probably end up doing many things improperly along the way.

This situation makes it difficult to determine "What are *Hashem's* real expectations of us? Does *Hashem* expect perfection or does He expect us to strive imperfectly, but generally do what is right and to improve over time? The מְסִילַת יְשָׁרִים seemed to be saying that *Hashem* really does expect and demand perfection. However, it seems that there are probably different ways to "expect perfection". On one hand the fact that it's theoretically possible to achieve perfection means that in a way there is a certain level of responsibility to be perfect. However, the fact that realistically even the greatest of people don't achieve perfection means that *Hashem* does not expect that we will be perfect. *Hashem* knows we are created in a way that we need to develop our character traits, that it takes time, and that we have powerful forces that pull us away from serving *Hashem*, and that we have endless responsibilities. We know that *Hashem* cares about us and that *Hashem* will not hold us accountable in a way that isn't realistic and appropriate. Therefore, it would seem that overall *Hashem's* expectations are for us to try to do our best to do the right thing as much as we can.

CHAPTER 13 - OUR JOB IS TO TRY, NOT TO CREATE RESULTS

אור ישראל - יז'
נודע כי אדם יולד לעמל ללחום מלחמת מצוה והחובה עליו להתייגע בעבודת
השם לא רק לשמור מה שטבעו מניחו בעצמו ומה שהוא קצת כבידות להזניח כי
בזה האופן אין האדם עובד השם רק הטבע עושה את שלה.

אור ישראל - ח'
נודע כי המצות נערכות נגד צער קיומם כמאמר חז"ל לפום צערא אגרא.

The אור ישראל explains that results don't define success when it comes to spiritual accomplishment and reward. Rather, working hard to overcome difficult challenges is the definition of success in עבודת השם. When we define accomplishment based upon results, we are not measuring our accomplishments properly. In עבודת ה' (as in all difficult, important things in life,) it is critical to have an accurate understanding and means of measuring success and failure.

Reb Dovid Leibowitz זצ"ל used to explain that since Hashem determines the results of all of our actions we are not responsible to create any specific outcome. Rather, our responsibility is to put in the effort to do a מצוה. The effort is in our control, and so our success is defined by this effort.

חידושי הלב על ספר שמות
פרשת בשלח ד"ה עוד מעט וסקלוני
ואני אמרתי לריק יגעתי. (ישעיה מט')
רד"ק: ואני אמרתי לריק יגעתי- בראותי כי לא שבו ישראל בתשובה בתוכחתי,
אמרתי לריק יגעתי. (והקב"ה השיב לו) וכי נקל הוא מהיותך לי עבד ולא די לך
בזה, אע"פ שלא ישמעו אליך אנשי דורך די לך שעשית שליחותי.
דברי הקב"ה לישעיה שאין להסיח דעת מהתכלית שהיא להיות עבד נאמן
לפניו, ולעשות את שליחותו, ואין נפקא מינה אם שליחותו מצליח או לא.

Hashem was reminding *Yeshaya Hanavi* that his only concern should be to perform the tasks that *Hashem* gives him. It's not relevant to *Yeshaya* whether his actions lead to results or not. A human being is only capable of putting in effort. We can't control the results. It's only our responsibility to try, and trying itself is our success.

אור הצפון - כח הבחירה
יסוד בזה, שעיקר רצונו של הקב"ה הוא שישתמשו בכח הבחירה, והפכו את הרע לטוב.

The אור הצפון explains how we should understand our mission in life. There are many things that need to be done in this world, and *Hashem* gives us the responsibility to take care of them: there are poor people who need food and shelter, sick people who need medicine, *shuls* and *yeshivas* that need to be built, there are people who need to be taught *Torah*, etc. The אור הצפון explains that our main responsibility is taking our human makeup and improving our inner being – "והפכו את הרע לטוב." Even though we live in a world where accomplishment is almost exclusively measured by tangible results, however, in עבודת ה' developing our inner character is the ultimate goal.

CHAPTER 14 - WE ALL HAVE OUR OWN INDIVIDUALIZED MISSION

Even though the same *Torah* was given to all the Jews, and in many ways, we all have the same mission, the same responsibilities, and the same expectations, we all also have a personalized mission with unique responsibilities and expectations. There are many aspects of individualized responsibilities.

גר"א משלי טז' ד'

לכל אדם ואדם יש לו דרך בפני עצמו לילך בו, כי אין דעתם דומין זה לזה, ואין טבע שני בני אדם שווים... דרכו אשר ילך בו לפי שורש נשמתו ולפי טבע גופו

מסילת ישרים - פרק כו' סוף הספר

דרך החסידות הראוי למי שתורתו אומנתו אינו דרך החסידות הראוי למי שצריך להשכיר עצמו למלאכת חבירו, ולא זה וזה דרך החסידות הראוי למי שעוסק בסחורתו. וכן כל שאר הפרטים אשר בעסקי האדם בעולם, כל אחד ואחד לפי מה שהוא ראויים לו דרכי החסידות. לא לפי שההחסידות משתנה כי הנה הוא שוה לכל נפש וודאי, הואיל ואיננו אלא לעשות מה שיש נחת רוח ליוצרו בו. אבל הואיל והנושאים משתנים אי אפשר שלא ישתנו האמצעים המגיעים אותם אל התכלית, כל אחד לפי ענינו.

The core mission to serve *Hashem* is the same for all people at all times. We all have been given the same 613 *mitzvos* and we have the same *sifrei halacha*. However, the way that we serve *Hashem* is unique to each individual, in each situation. The גר"א and the מסילת ישרים explain that our character and our experiences in life dictate what the proper service of *Hashem* will be. Our serving *Hashem* includes all our thoughts, feelings, words, and behaviors, therefore every nuance in our lives is a part of the equation. Because the factors in our lives are different, and our physical, emotional, and psychological natures are all different, if we are doing the same things as each other, it's likely that we are not doing the proper thing. The גר"א says that even the natures of our נשמות are different.

All these differences cause us to have different paths in our spiritual journey.

One example that the מסילת ישרים discusses is about the type of job that a person chooses. There are situations when it's appropriate for a person to spend most of his day learning *Torah* and not earning a *parnasah*, and there are situations when someone should be working and not learning. Some of those people who work should be working for themselves and some should be employees of others, some should be in specific fields in specific positions. *Hashem* has different roles for different people. The מסילת ישרים explains that a person's particular job has a significant impact on his appropriate *Avodas Hashem*. It's obvious when you think about it, but we manage not to think about it too much.

<u>חובות הלבבות - שער הבטחון ג</u>

מי שהוא מבני אדם חזק בגופו וחלש בהכרתו ראוי לו מהם שיש בו מן היגיעה
כפי שיכול לסבול, ומי שהוא חלש בגופו ובהכרתו חזקה אל יבקש מסיבות
הטרף מה שמגיע גופו אך יטה אל מה שיהיה קל על גופו ויוכל להתמיד עליו.
ולכל אדם יש חפץ במלאכה או סחורה מבלתי זולתה, כבר הטביע הקל לה
בטבעו אהבה וחבה. וכן בשאר החיים כמו שהטביע בטבע החתול צידת
העכברים, ובטבע הנץ צידת מה שראוי לו מן העוף, ובטבע האיל צידת
הנחשים, וכן יש מן העופות שיצודו הדגים לבד. וכן בטבע מין ומין ממיני
החיים נטיה ותאוה אל מין ממיני הצמחים והחיים, הוטבע עליו להיות סיבה
למזונו, ותכונת גופו ואבריו ראויין לדבר ההוא כפה הארוך והשוק הארוך לעוף
שהוא צד את הדגים... ועל הדמיון הזה תמצא מדות בני אדם וגופתם מוכנות
לסחורות ולמלאכות. ומי שמוציא במידותיו וטבעו כוסף אל מלאכה מהמלאכות
ויהיה גופו ראוי לה ויוכל לסבול את טרחה יחזור עליה.

The חובות הלבבות explains that *Hashem* gives us each our own individualized mission in a very personalized way. He explains that when we think about the nature of animals, we can see that different animals have different needs, and we can also see that *Hashem* built in to their nature the skills, the physical properties, and the inclination for them to get what they need. *Hashem* created lions with a need to eat meat and *Hashem* also created them with the tools to be able to get the meat. There are many factors that make it easier for us to succeed in one type of job more than another. *Hashem* specifically gave us each our own specific nature and circumstances and He wants us to follow the path that fits with our nature and our circumstances.

<u>אור ישראל - איגרת ג</u>

תלמוד תורה -קשי יום וחסרי דעת במצוקות רעות יש מקום לפוטרם, איש איש לפי ענינו ישולל מחיובם, לא ראי זה כראי זה, כל אשר ירחיב לאדם כן יגדל החיוב

One example how our different responsibilities כלפי מעלה play out relates to our חיוב to learn תורה. Learning *Torah* is perhaps the most important *Mitzva* (תלמוד תורה כנגד כולם). However, *Reb Yisroel* explains that every person's responsibilities to learn *Torah* are different in type, time, and trial. For example, a person's energy level and state of mind (among other factors) affects their ability and, therefore, their responsibility, to learn. There are some people whose responsibility to learn *Torah* may be little or even none at times.

<u>אור ישראל - איגרת ו</u>

בכל פרט העבירה נבדלים בני האדם זה מזה בקבלת עונשם לפי תכונתם ומצבם בעוה"ז; עני ועשיר, חכם וסכל, זריז ועצל בטבעו. וכיוצא הרבה והרבה בחינות שונות...באותו אדם בעצמו, באותו פרט חלק מן העבירה עצמה, נבדל בעונשה לפי התחלפות תכונת מצבו, מעת המנוחה לעת הטרדה, מתכונת המנוחה לתכונת הטרדה, מתכונת שקטת הרעיון לתכונת בלבול הרעיון, וכיוצא בחינות מתחלפות הרבה, וכל אשר תקל לפני האדם להישמר מן העבירה. כן תגדל ענשו.

Reb Yisroel explains that every person has a different situation in life. Our nature, our experiences, our assets, and our limitations are all different. We have different financial situations, intellectual capacities, character traits, together with so many other differences. Within each person's life, often even at different times in the course of a single day, there are so many factors which affect our capacity, where our abilities and challenges are different.

Reb Yisroel tells us that *Hashem's* expectations of us change based upon our changing circumstances. *Hashem* is aware of the different internal and external factors in our lives, and these alter accordingly His expectations for us. When it is easy for us to do a certain מצוה or to overcome a particular challenge, *Hashem's* expectation increases.

Hashem has a different mission for each of us. He created each of us very intentionally very differently, and *Hashem* intended each of us to have a different mission with different challenges and goals.

CHAPTER 15 - SPIRITUAL SUCCESS = DOING OUR BEST TO SUCCEED AT OUR PERSONAL MISSION

The way we define spiritual success is obviously based on how we understand our spiritual mission. In all endeavors, especially hard ones, we must have a clear understanding of our goal and therefore of success. For example, when running a marathon, if you're not sure if you are supposed to run 2.62 miles, 26.2 miles, or 262 miles, the marathon will be very difficult to finish. When you are at 26.1 miles and you're not sure if you have a tenth of a mile left or 235.9 miles left, it's particularly beneficial to know where the finish line is. This is an oversimplification, but the reality is that many of us struggle with having an accurate understanding of what our own spiritual success ought to look like.

Here are some common mistakes: 1) Expecting perfection. 2) Expecting immediate results. 3) Measuring success based upon results. 4) Having the same expectations for all people or measuring one's success against the perceived performance of another person.

We must realize that it's not realistic for us to be perfect, and it's certainly not realistic for us to be perfect immediately. Even more importantly, it's not our job to create results. Rather, we have to try our best to do the right thing. Remember, every person's mission in life is unique and individualized, and our responsibilities can be vastly different from another person's.

Many of the misconceptions about what our mission is in life comes from the fact that our job in life is that we should be a righteous person. However, when many of us think about what a righteous person is, we often have a specific image in our minds; usually it is perfection and always doing the right thing. The type of accomplishments that we often think of when we are thinking about the ideal righteous man are tangible and visible accomplishments. Those are the ones that stand out and they seem to be very special. When we think about areas of עבודת ה' such as learning *Torah*, davening to *Hashem*, doing *mitzvos*, or having good *middos*, we may expect to be like the *Chofetz Chaim* or *Rav Moshe*. They (seemingly) were able to learn without interruption, had complete faith in *Hashem*, did all the *mitzvos* properly, and had perfect *middos*. We may think that being like the חפץ חיים is a good goal for us, but it's important to understand that our job is merely to try our best with who we are and the situation in life *Hashem* has put us in.

Similarly, we may think that we are expected to create results with our actions. However, the reality is that *Hashem* is in charge of all of the results in this world. When we try our best, we are achieving success even when we are not perfect and even when we don't see tangible results. *Hashem* gives everyone different strengths and different challenges. *Hashem's* expectations are different for each of us based upon the conglomerate of the many aspects of our lives. We must understand that when we do the best we can, when we sincerely try to serve *Hashem*, we are fulfilling our spiritual mission and achieving our ultimate spiritual success.

CHAPTER 16 - THE BENEFITS OF HAVING AN ACCURATE DEFINITION OF SPIRITUAL SUCCESS

The question we ask ourselves, "Am I acting as a good person?" or, "Is my friend acting as a good person?" is necessarily dependent upon our understanding of what a good person is. Our self-respect and our respect for others is likewise dependent on our definition of what it means to be a good person. A more precise appellation for being a "good person" is to be a spiritually successful person; and so, our perception of ourselves and others, and of our perception of others' perception of ourselves, is determined by how we define spiritual success.

If we equate success with either perfection or with tangible results, then we will limit our ability to consider ourselves or others as being successful. We will often consider ourselves or others to be bad people, and we will not be able to have respect or self-respect. However, when we have an appropriate definition of success, which is measured by how we work with who and what we are, then we have a greater ability to consider ourselves or others to be good, spiritually successful, and deserving of great respect.

The way that we measure success and failure also affects many of our decisions in life. For example, the goals that we set for ourselves are necessarily arrived at by our definition of success. Similarly, the goals we set for our children and the way we try to raise/teach them are formulated on the same basis.

CHAPTER 17 - CREATING APPROPRIATE/REALISTIC EXPECTATIONS FOR OURSELVES (AND WHY THAT'S IMPORTANT)

It's important to not underestimate our responsibilities, capabilities, and opportunities. It's also important to not overestimate our responsibilities, capabilities, and opportunities. The expectations we create for ourselves affect the goals we set for ourselves, and these in turn affect our sense of accomplishment and self-respect.

As we wrote in previous chapters, *Hashem* created the entire world for our benefit - בשבילי נברא העולם. *Hashem's* goal was to give us the opportunity to receive the ultimate good - להתענג על השם, as a result of fulfilling our responsibilities in this world. That we have a chance to receive this reward for doing the *mitzvos* means that we have great opportunities. That *Hashem* gave us this opportunity, and that he is constantly sustaining us and helping us in our lives creates, as well, a tremendous responsibility for us to keep His *mitzvos*.

When we appreciate the importance of doing the *mitzvos* and how beneficial it is for us to keep them, we will be motivated to do our best to keep the *mitzvos* properly. Additionally, when we know that our actions are important, for ourselves and for the universe, and when we understand that *mitzvos* are responsibilities as well as opportunities, we will pursue the *mitzvos* with happiness and enthusiasm; we are generally much more positive and productive when we feel like our job is important.

Even when we appreciate how beneficial it is to do as many *mitzvos* as we can, we will generally only attempt to accomplish what we feel we can accomplish. Therefore, if we underestimate our capabilities we are likely to limit the amount we attempt to accomplish.

It may seem, in a way, that overestimating our responsibilities and capabilities is not a bad thing. It follows that the more we think we can do the more we will be motivated to work hard to accomplish as much as we can. There is some truth to that; however, there are also problems that can come from overestimating our capabilities or our responsibilities.

One example of this is brought down by the מסילת ישרים in פרק יג where he writes that when people are striving for extreme spiritual achievement, they can neglect their basic physical needs. The מ"י explains that even though the person may be sincerely motivated to serve *Hashem*, his inappropriate asceticism isn't helpful for his overall spirituality. People need their needs to be met to function properly. The person may think that he is not only capable, but responsible to maintain a certain lofty lifestyle. However, the מסילת ישרים explains, when a person is not on the appropriate level for a certain type of spiritual behavior, it's not helpful and therefore, it's not even proper.

The מסילת ישרים in the הקדמה refers to another type of overestimating our capabilities. He explains that most people think that they are knowledgeable about the fundamental aspects of serving *Hashem*. They think they understand what *Hashem* wants from us and they think that they understand the proper methods of spiritual growth. However, the reality is that most people overestimate their spiritual מדרגה and capabilities because they don't understand the fundamental basics of serving *Hashem*. We need to learn what *Hashem* really wants from us. The מ"י writes that we have much work to do in very basic areas of understanding *Hashem's* priorities for us.

The way that we are likely to feel about ourselves when we overestimate our responsibilities includes feelings of guilt, shame, and hopelessness. By contrast, when we live up to what we think our responsibilities are, we feel good about ourselves.

When we overestimate what we are supposed to be doing to serve *Hashem*, we will inevitably fall short of these expectations. Consequently, we will feel we have not lived up to our responsibilities and we will feel guilty. We will think we are not doing the right thing, that there is something wrong with us, that we are bad. Because we have overestimated ourselves, we will not be able to accomplish the tasks we set for ourselves even when we try our hardest. Eventually we may attempt to do something extreme in our effort to live up to our expectations, or we will give up when we see we cannot achieve what we have set out to accomplish. The result is that we will see ourselves as failures. This leads to overall feelings of not being worthwhile, to being embarrassed, and to being crushed.

CHAPTER 18 - HOW TO DEVELOP APPROPRIATE EXPECTATIONS

There are many things to consider when we attempt to determine appropriate expectations for ourselves:

• What is the *ideal* of what should be accomplished?

• What is *realistic* for what can be accomplished?

• How *important* is it for these things to be accomplished?

• What are the *ramifications* if these goals are or are not accomplished?

The *Torah's* expectations for people are very much related to each individual's unique strengths and challenges. To accurately ascertain what *Hashem* wants from us, we need to understand the *Torah's* general objective expectations, we must also understand people's general strengths and weaknesses and how they relate to the *Torah's* rules. Then, we need to understand what our specific strengths and weaknesses are and to see how that relates to *Hashem's* expectations for us.

Each of these points requires thought and wisdom and effort to understand.

CHAPTER 19 - CLARITY ABOUT HASHEM'S PURPOSE FOR PEOPLE, THE WORLD, AND THE TORAH LEADS TO AN ACCURATE UNDERSTANDING OF HASHEM

Even after a person recognizes that there is a God who created the world, he must still determine - *Who is this God? What is His nature? Is He someone who will be helpful to me, Is He someone who I can have a relationship with? Is He someone who I want to have a relationship with? Is He someone who I need to listen to? Is He someone who I want to listen to? Is He someone I want to emulate?*

Unfortunately, many people do not have the true understanding about these matters, and that affects their entire approach to their relationship with *Hashem*, and with spirituality as a whole. There are people who have an impression of God that he is egocentric; that he needs people to recognize him, to serve him, and to appreciate him; and that he gets angry, jealous, and vengeful when people don't listen properly. Overall many people view *Hashem* as unkind or as a harsh, even cruel dictator. When someone has these impressions about *Hashem*, then their relationship with *Hashem* revolves around these perspectives. This leads people to resent *Hashem*, and when they do listen to *Hashem*, they are listening without really appreciating it.

God is also often thought of as being not understanding. He is thought to have very high and seemingly unrealistic expectations of us, and to be very critical of us and of our mistakes.

Similarly, even after we have the knowledge that *Hashem* gave us the *Torah*, that *Hashem* gave us the *mitzvos*, and that we must keep the *mitzvos*, even though we may acknowledge that reward and punishment are attached to our keeping the *Torah* and the *mitzvos*, we must still determine – *Why did Hashem give us these mitzvos? What is the purpose of the mitzvos? What is the nature of the mitzvos? Are the mitzvos good for us?*

Unfortunately, in these areas as well, many people, many *frum* Jews who have been raised in *yeshivos* and have learned *Torah* their whole lives don't have a true understanding, and that causes their approach to the *Torah* and *mitzvos* to be distorted and unproductive. Many people have the impression that the *mitzvos* are a set of rules whose purpose is for *Hashem's* personal benefit, and that the *mitzvos* are not necessarily good for us. Or, some people are under the impression that because *Hashem* would like us to do the *mitzvos*, he created a system of reward and punishment in order to encourage us to serve him.

Others are generally unsure what the purpose is for the *mitzvos*. this also leads to a less productive form of serving *Hashem*.

However, when we have the true understanding of what *Hashem's* purpose was for creating the world, for creating us, and for giving us the *Torah*, it gives us the true perspective on some of these matters,

It gives us an accurate understanding about who *Hashem* is.

When it's clear to us that *Hashem* created the entire world just for the purpose of doing *chessed* for us, we come to understand the giving nature of *Hashem*. We also come to understand that everything that *Hashem* does for us and for others is in the context of *chessed*. If a person doesn't know why *Hashem* created people, and what *Hashem's* purpose was in creating the world, then his understanding of the nature of *Hashem* and the intent of *Hashem's* actions will be distorted and incorrect.

It also helps our relationship with *Hashem*.

When we realize how much *Hashem* loves us and cares about us, and how much *Hashem* does and has done for us, then we can develop a sense of appreciation toward *Hashem*. We can also develop feelings of love and awe for *Hashem*.

It helps us realize that the purpose of *Hashem* giving us the *Mitzvos* is for our benefit.

When we work hard to serve *Hashem* it is good for us. The *mitzvos* are opportunities for us to be involved in matters that will be beneficial for us. They help us to become better people and they help us to be able to merit the greatest benefits. When we realize the benefits of the *Torah* and the *mitzvos*, it affects our attitude toward the *mitzvos*. We can sometimes feel that, "I have to do the *mitzvos*, but it would be much better for me if I didn't have to do them." When we understand that doing the *mitzvos* gets us to the ultimate good, we will have a much more positive attitude about them.

It becomes clear to us that *Hashem* cares about us despite our failures.

Hashem certainly would not create expectations for us that are not realistic, and He would not ignore the difficulties that are involved in keeping the *mitzvos*. Rather, the expectations are custom tailored for what is best for our spiritual growth.

The fact that *Hashem* created us for the purpose of giving us the greatest good, and the fact that *Hashem* created the entire world and runs the entire world in order to help us achieve that good, and the fact that the *mitzvos* were given to us as a gift in order to help us, affects our approach toward doing *mitzvos* in nearly every conceivable way. Both our responsibility and our desire to follow the instructions of *Hashem* come from the recognition of how much *Hashem* has done for us. We are responsible to listen due to the good that we have received, and we want to listen to the One who has helped us so much. We also want to listen when we recognize that everything is all for our own benefit. Our love for *Hashem*, our awe of *Hashem*, and our fear of *Hashem* also come from the recognition of how much *Hashem* has done for us and in general, and how much *Hashem* is in control of our personal future and that of the entire world.

It leads to clarity about the purpose of human suffering.

Another significant benefit that comes as a result of realizing that *Hashem's* whole purpose for the world, for people, and for the *Torah*, is only for our benefit, is that it clarifies the context of how to view suffering and the challenges people experience in this world. It becomes clear that *Hashem* is loving, caring, and generous. Therefore, the reason that people suffer is not because *Hashem* doesn't care, or because *Hashem* is out to hurt people. Even those who don't follow the *Torah* aren't getting punished because *Hashem* has decided to be mean to them. Rather, the punishments, like everything else we have shown, from love and a loving purpose, and from a loving God.

The recognition that human suffering is part of *Hashem's* plan, and that *Hashem's* plan is intertwined with *chessed*, can help us to have a good relationship with *Hashem*. This understanding can lead us to be motivated to keep the *mitzvos*, and it can help us to find meaning in the difficult experiences in our lives.

<u>שבת קכז.</u>
אמר רב יהודה אמר רב גדולה הכנסת אורחין מהקבלת פני שכינה דכתיב ויאמר
ה' אם נא מצאתי חן בעיניך אל נא תעבור וכו'

There is a story in the *Torah* that clarifies to us how to understand who *Hashem* is and what *Hashem's* priorities are. In the beginning of *Parshas Vayeira*, *Avraham* had a unique opportunity. *Hashem* had come to visit him and *Hashem* was having a conversation with him. In the meantime, *Avraham* noticed that there were three men who were on the road and they needed food and shelter. *Avraham* told *Hashem* that he needed to take a break from the conversation to tend to the guests.

Hashem is often described as a king and a master. In general, if a slave is having a special meeting with his master, or if a subject is having a special meeting with his king, and the slave or subject informs the king or the master that he wants to take a break from the meeting in order to tend to someone else's needs, the king would be furious. Such an action would show a massive lack of respect for the king or the master, and a disregard for their wishes. It's hard to understand why *Avraham* decided to take a break from a discussion with *Hashem* for the purpose of helping a few random strangers. This would seem to be a lack of respect for *Hashem*, and it would seem to be against *Hashem's* wishes. And yet we know that *Avraham's* priorities in life were to bring honor to *Hashem* and to respect *Hashem's* wishes.

Not only did *Avraham* make this decision, it is also the *halacha* (רמב"ם הלכות אבל פרק י"ד הלכה ב'). We see from the גמרא and from the רמב"ם that it was *Hashem's* desire for *Avraham* to take a break from their meeting to tend to the other people's needs. How could such a thing be appropriate?

There are two potential scenarios when a king or a master would be happy if their subject or their slave would interrupt their meeting to tend to someone else's needs.

One situation would be where the person who is in need is someone who the king or the master cares about enough in order for him to want the subject or the slave to stop the meeting in order to tend to that person's needs. For example; if the king's child or the master's child is starving and needs shelter on a hot day, then it's understood that it's appropriate to stop the meeting and to provide food and shelter for the child. It's both what is desired by the king or master and is therefore the appropriate display of respect as well. We know that *Hashem* is described as אבינו מלכינו, the father and the king of the Jewish people - *Hashem* tells us in the *Torah* בנים אתם לה' אלוקיכם. *Hashem* is our king and we must treat him as a king. However, *Hashem* is also our father. *Hashem* loves everyone as it says in *Pirkei Avos*: חביב אדם שנברא בצלם. When *Avraham* saw the travelers, who needed to be taken care of, he knew that *Hashem* loved these travelers and therefore, he knew that *Hashem* would want them to be taken care of so much that it was clear to *Avraham* that *Hashem* would want him to stop their meeting to tend to the guests.

Another type of situation when a king or master would want his subject or servant to interrupt a meeting with the king or master is if the servant or subject has been given a specific mission or specific responsibilities by the king or master. Then if the mission needed to be done at the time of the meeting with the king, then, if the mission is really important to the king, the king may want the mission to be done even if it means that his servant must interrupt the meeting. So too, *Avraham* knew that חסד is so important to *Hashem* that *Hashem* would want him to do the חסד even if it means breaking off a meeting with *Hashem*.

This clarifies to us how much *Hashem* loves all people and how much *Hashem* wants everyone to be taken care of. Obviously, *Hashem* is not interested in people serving Him for the sake of His ego because if that was the case, it would have angered *Hashem* for *Avraham* to stop the meeting for the purpose of helping others!

CHAPTER 20 - REALIZING THAT HASHEM GAVE US AN IMPORTANT MISSION IN LIFE IS EXTREMELY BENEFICIAL.

There are many benefits to realizing that we have a purpose in this world, that our purpose is a mission given to us by *Hashem*, and that our mission has great value, and is extremely important.

Unfortunately, some people live their lives without a focus on pursuing the mission *Hashem* gave them.
Instead, their pursuits revolve around honor, fame, power, pleasure, or comforts. These types of pursuits can lead a person to temporary feelings of happiness and success. However, when a person asks himself "What have I really accomplished with my life?" he will often recognize that he hasn't been successful in a meaningful way. This is because we can only feel a real sense of accomplishment when we have done something that has moral or ethical value. At times, we don't have these perspectives clear; either because we aren't focused properly, or because we don't want to see the truth, or because our vision has been distorted. As a result, we spend our powers getting things, oftentimes giving away our lives, for things with no value.

The reality is that *Hashem* created us and He gave us opportunities and responsibilities. This is true regardless of whether we realize this or not. When we are aware of this reality and we take it seriously, then we can pursue these opportunities and responsibilities with ambition and receive great benefit. However, when we don't realize the truth, or even when we merely don't focus on the truth, it leads us to squandering our opportunities and neglecting our responsibilities.

תפילת שחרית

ברוך הוא אלוקינו שבראנו לכבודו..והבדילנו מן הטועים, ונתן לנו תורת אמת
וחיי עולם נטע בתוכנו. הוא יפתח לבנו בתורתו וישם בלבנו אהבתו ויראתו
ולעשות רצונו ולעבדו בלבב שלם למען לא ניגע לריק ולא נלד לבהלה

In ובא לציון we thank *Hashem* for helping us recognize and
understand that *Hashem* runs the world, and that our true,
meaningful, and productive mission is to follow *Hashem's Torah*
instead of spending our lives being "ניגע לריק" -working hard for
little or no benefit, and living our lives "לבהלה" -with no purpose.
When a person doesn't have the proper understanding of where to
invest his time, money, and energy, he can spend his entire life
working hard without really accomplishing anything meaningful.

מסילת ישרים - פרק ב

ההולך בעולמו בלי התבוננות אם טובה דרכו או רעה, הנה הוא כסומא ההולך על
שפת הנהר, אשר סכנתו וודאי עצומה, ורעתו קרובה לבא

The מסילת ישרים is alerting us to the fact that we have many
responsibilities, regardless of whether we are aware of them, and
that we can easily neglect them (especially if we are not aware of
them), just as in a situation when someone is walking on the side of
the river, he is in danger of falling in, and that danger is even
greater if he isn't aware of the fact that he is on the side of the
river. So too, we must be aware of our responsibilities, and we need
to be alert and focused in order to not fall into the trap of
neglecting our responsibilities and not taking advantage of our
opportunities.

We have an extremely important purpose in this world. The value in
our mission is something we can appreciate. Furthermore, our
mission, if undertaken sincerely, is one that will bring us
tremendous happiness and satisfaction. The more we realize this,
the more we will be motivated to pursue that mission, and the
more success we will find.

אין אנו מכירין גדולתו של האדם...לכן כל יגיעתינו והשגותינו מצומצמות, ואין אנו מוצאים איפוא ביגיעתינו אלא רק בהתאם למושגינו...אם כן, זוהי חובת האדם להתבונן ולהכיר מהו ערכו.

We generally are motivated, persistent, and passionate about matters that we see as significant and important. When we see a situation where we are able to accomplish an extremely important goal, then, we are ready, willing, and able to put in the effort that is necessary to accomplish matters that are very difficult.

Hashem created us in a way that we don't naturally understand how important that our responsibilities and opportunities are. That leads us to not have the appreciation for the significance in our lives, and as a result, we don't fulfill our responsibilities appropriately. One of our most basic and most important responsibilities that we have, is to work on understanding and appreciating our significance and the significance of our actions, and acting accordingly.

נבראים ומתחדשים עבור כל יחיד כל העולמות.
כל אדם נברא בצלם אלוקים, וכל אחד לבדו יש בו תכלית היצירה כולה.

The entire world is created for the benefit of every person. This gives us a perspective on the importance and the significance of each person and for the mission of each one of them.

Chapter 21 - We Have an Important Mission for Every Moment in Our Lives

חולין-ז:

"אין עוד מלבדו"-אמר רבי חנינא ואפילו כשפים. רש"י-שאם אין גזירה
מלפניו אין מריעין לו לאדם.
אמר רבי חנינא אין אדם נוקף אצבעו למעלה אא"כ מכריזים עליו מלמעלה.

It is common for a person to think that even if we were designed by *Hashem* for an important reason, and our lives overall have significance, however, the details of our lives are not really important. This will often lead a person to view the details of our lives as annoying and frustrating. We will often not see the value in dealing with the details of our lives in a productive and appropriate way.

Hashem controls every single thing in our lives. Everything that happens to us is for a reason. There is a purpose to everything that we experience in our lives. We also have a responsibility to act appropriately at every moment, and to deal with everything in our lives in an appropriate fashion. This means that every moment in our lives has a purpose, and every moment is an opportunity for us to achieve something great. It also means that we can look at every situation that we have in life as an opportunity that was specifically designed by *Hashem* for our benefit as an opportunity to help us to succeed. This can give us an optimistic view of every situation that we have in our lives, and it can help us to make the best of every moment that we have.

אור הצפון מלעיל

שנדע איך להעריך את האדם ואת כל רגע ורגע בחייו...ואם נדע את הסוד הזה
נוכל להגיע למדרגות עליונות ולמטרת המין האנושי...אבל אין אנו מכירים

גדולתו של האדם ואין מבין את ערכו של רגע...לכן כל יגיעתינו והשגותינו
מצומצמות ואין אנו מוצאים ביגיעתינו אלא רק בהתאם למושגינו.

The *Alter* teaches us that we are motivated to accomplish when we
realize that our lives are important and that our actions are
important. However, even after we recognize that our lives and our
actions are important, if we think that only certain actions in our
lives are important, then we will only be motivated to excel in those
areas. Also, we will not value our accomplishments that we have
except in certain areas, as opposed to realizing that there are many
different areas that are important and we are responsible to
accomplish in these areas, and we are capable to accomplish in
these areas. There will always be many opportunities to accomplish
in our lives. Every moment of our lives presents an opportunity to
accomplish something of great significance!

CHAPTER 22 - WE NEED AN ACCURATE UNDERSTANDING OF OUR TRUE MISSION

Even after a person has recognized that *Hashem* gave us the *Torah* and that our overall mission is to do the *mitzvos*, the specifics of our mission can sometimes be difficult to determine. It is extremely important for us to understand our mission in life in a precise, specific, accurate, practical, personal, comprehensive way.

The reason that it's important to have clarity about our mission from *Hashem* is because it doesn't work to serve *Hashem* in a way that isn't appropriate even if we are sincerely trying to do the right thing.

אור ישראל - אגרת ד
הגם שהתורה מסורה לבני אדם לחתוך עניינה כפי מטרת שכל האנושי. לא נכבשה היא לעשות בה כחפצינו על פי תהלוכות רצונינו

The *Torah* gives us the guidelines/instructions for what we should be doing. However, *Hashem* gave the *Torah* to humans, and it was with the understanding that in many situations we will be unable to figure out what Hashem really wants us to do, what would the true dictate of the *Torah* in this situation. *Hashem* only expects us to do our best to try to figure out what He wants us to do. However, *Reb Yisroel Salanter* is warning us that it is not good enough for us to follow "what we think is best", without trying to verify whether we are doing the proper עבודת ה'. Part of our mission is to constantly work to the best of our ability with all of the resources available to us to understand the רצון ה'.

מסילת ישרים - הקדמה
מאלה וממאלה יחסר חסידות האמיתי ויהיה יקר מאד למצא אותו בעולם. כי יחסר מן החכמים למיעוט עיונם בו ויחסר מן הבלתי חכמים למיעוט השגתם אותו עד

שידמו רוב בני האדם שההסידות תלוי באמירת מזמורים הרבה וידויים ארוכים
מאד צומות קשים וטבילות קרח ושלג. כלם דברים שאין השכל נח בהם ואין
הדעת שוקטה, וחסידות האמיתי הנרצה והנחמד רחוק מציור שכלינו.
אך האמת הוא כי עיון גדול צריך על כל הדברים האלה לדעת אותם באמת ולא
על צד הדמיון והסברה הכוזבת.

It's often difficult to determine the proper עבודת ה' in general and in
specific situations. The מסילת ישרים tells us that (besides for the
tremendous work required to learn and understand the great
amount of תורה necessary to properly perform the external הלכות,)
great study is necessary in order to understand the proper עבודה
שבלב. He further adds that most people have such a distorted
understanding that it causes them to do very strange things as their
עבודת ה'. The מסילת ישרים tells us that we are responsible to do our
best to develop our knowledge of the *Torah* in order to better
understand what is proper and what isn't.

CHAPTER 23 - THE TORAH AND MITZVOS ARE THE GUIDE, THE PATH, AND THE GOAL OF OUR MISSION.

The *Torah* and the *Mitzvos* Are Specifically Designed to Assist Us (as humans, with Human Nature), to Develop Ourselves. They Help Us to Develop Our Greatness and to Deal with Our Vulnerability.

The *Torah* contains several different areas of guidance for us: the enumerated *mitzvos*, ideals and values, and the wisdom of *Hashem*.

What are the *mitzvos*?

The *mitzvos* are a set of rules and guidelines based upon the *Torah's* ideals and values that reveal the way *Hashem* wants us to live, and therefore, also, they highlight the path towards a successful and happy life.

On the surface, it may seem that the *mitzvos* are not specifically connected to a person's nature and predicament in עוֹלָם הזה, but are, rather, guidelines and commands that are based on objective principles and realities of the universe. It would seem that the *Torah* tells us what the proper behaviors are, and the *Torah* teaches us that we are held responsible to follow these instructions.

In truth, the *Torah* doesn't merely "Define What Is the Ultimate Good" and instruct us to "Be Good". Rather, the *Torah* and the *Mitzvos* work with who we are. They teach us about the process of Human Development, and through the process of keeping the *mitzvos* we can develop our character properly.

התורה כולה, כל מצוותיה והלכותיה, משקפת במוחו של המין האנושי... כיצד עליו להתנהג, ומה יש לו לעשות בעולמו.

As the *Alter* writes, the *Torah* was specifically designed to be a guide, to assist and instruct a person to develop himself and realize his fullest potential and the fullest potential of his existence in this world with all the challenges and difficulties of life.

משה רבינו explained to the מלאכים (in the *Midrash* we brought down in chapter 6) that it is clear from the תורה that it was created by *Hashem* for humanity for our מצב in עולם הזה:

כלום אתם עושים מלאכה, שאתם צריכים שבות? משא ומתן יש ביניכם? אב ואם יש לכם? קנאה יש לכם? יצר הרע יש ביניכם?

The מצות that are in the תורה are directly related to the human experience in עולם הזה; to our challenges and weaknesses, our needs and interests. משה explained that it is clear that the תורה is designed for people in עולם הזה from the fact that so much of the תורה is directly connected to the human experience in עוה"ז. Along with its didactic dimension, meaning the facts or details about the מצות, the תורה is the vehicle through which a person can accomplish his mission to grow spiritually and to serve *Hashem*. (And without the *Torah*, it is impossible to accomplish this mission.)

The *Mitzvos* Are Designed For Us With Our Physical Needs and Limitations and We are not Expected to be Perfect

ספר החינוך - שעד'

מוכרח על כל פנים לנטות מעבודת בוראו... ולהשתדל בצרכי הבית אשר ידור שם, כי לא יתקיים הבית, מבלתי שישגיח האדם עליו... לא יטוש מלאכת הבית לגמרי, גם זה יחשב לו עון... דכתיב "ויהי אדם לנפש חיה"... נשמה שנתתי בך... החיה... אל תהי צדיק הרבה... למה תשומם. יבא כפרה על עצמו (חטאת)... ראוי לו להביא כפרה על נפשו, כי אולי נוטה מן הגדר המחויב עליו בעניין גופו ונשמתו, כי שמא טבעו ודינינו נכון על צד שהנזירות עינוי יותר מדי על נפשו

The תורה creates a מצוה that a person needs to take care of his health. He must make sure to function properly as a human in order to serve 'ה.

This is an example of the מצות of the תורה being designed not only to help a person to develop his שכל. But even to help him take care of his גוף/גשמיות in עוה"ז. (Because taking care of our גוף properly is also needed in order to help us to serve 'ה.)

The מצות are given to help the person to find the proper balance between his גוף and his נשמה. A human is complicated as far as how to deal with ourselves in the proper way to serve 'ה. It's difficult to have the right balance, with the proper focus on the גוף and the proper focus on the נשמה. The מצות help us find this balance

מסילת ישרים - פרק יג

לא גזרו חכמים גזרה אא"כ רוב הציבור יכול לעמוד בו, אין רוב הציבור יכולים להיות חסידים... וכל מה שהוא מוכרח לו מאיזה טעם שיהיה, כיון שהוא מוכרח לו, אם הוא פורש ממנו, הרי זה חטא.

The מסילת ישרים explains that there are advantages to only pursuing areas of spirituality, and there are dangers to pursuing our physical needs and desires. Therefore, in a way, it would seem proper for there to be a prohibition against the pursuit of these matters. However, the *Torah* doesn't prohibit them because the *Torah* works with the understanding that we often need to pursue our physical pleasures, and therefore, it's appropriate to pursue them.

חובות הלבבות שער עבודות אלוקים פרק ב

אך הצורך המביא אל כל חלק מחלקי ההערה הוא מפני שההערה התקועה בשכל נחלשת משלשה פנים, התחייבונו לחזקה בהערה התוריה. ומפני שהיו ההנאות הגופיות קודמות אל נפש האדם מנעוריו וצוותו בהם מתחלת ענינו חזק, וגדול ונחזק בם יותר, הגבירה מדת התאוה על שאר מדותיו עד שגברה על השכל שנוצר עליו האדם וטחה מראות עיניו ואבדו סימני חמודתיו. והוצרך האדם בעבור זה לדברים שהם חוץ לו לעמוד בהם כנגד מדתו המגונה והיא התאוה להנאות הבהמיות ולהחיות בהם סימני מדתו המשובחת והוא השכל.

The חובות הלבבות writes that, left to his natural devices, a person will be overwhelmed with his physical needs and desires.

In fact, we see in the world all around us that people who don't have *Torah* in their lives in a meaningful way become entrenched and mired in the insatiable appetite for הבלי עולם הזה. *Hashem* gave us the תורה so that we can overcome the default nature of our human condition, and our נשמה/שכל can be the controlling force in our lives instead of our physical or automatic inclinations.

The ספר החינוך explains that the מצות of the תורה are designed in a way that works together with a human being's many facets in order to help him develop. The חינוך explains that a human being is extremely complicated by nature. The מצות are designed to work with all the human complexities in order to help us develop properly.

ספר החינוך מצוה שעד' (נזיר)
בכל עת שיוכל למעט בעבודת החומר, וישים מגמתו לעבודת קונו אז טוב לו.

מסילת ישרים פרק יג (נזיר)
כל הרואה סוטה בקלקולה, יזיר עצמו מן היין... כל ענייני העולם ניסיונות לאדם... רוב חולשת האדם וקרבת דעתו אל הרעות, כל מה שיוכל האדם להימלט... ראוי שיעשהו כדי שיהיה נשמר יותר מן הרעה אשר ברגליהם.

The מצוה of נזיר teaches us the principle that involvement in the pleasures of עולם הזה creates a potential challenge in the future to doing מצות and not doing עבירות. A person's nature is drawn toward his desires. This tendency is difficult to resist regardless of consequence or context.

Therefore, the *Torah* guides us to minimize our involvement in fulfilling our physical pleasures, which weakens the strength of their power over us and allows us to focus on our spiritual pursuits.

The *Mitzvos* Change Us and They Develop Our Greatness

A different concept about the nature and purpose of the *mitzvos* is described by the ספר החינוך:

ספר החינוך

(צה') – שהכל (מצות ALL OF THE) ... מחשבות כולם מטהרות... לטהר שם מחשבות בני איש ולתקן לבבם.

(טז') – האדם נפעל לפי פעולותיו, ולבו וכל מחשבותיו תמיד אחר מעשיו שהוא עוסק בהם... רצה הקב"ה לזכות את ישראל... תורה ומצות כדי להתפיס בהם כל מחשבותיו, כי מתוך הפעולות הטובים, אנחנו נפעלים להיות טובים.

The ספר החינוך is explaining that the overall mission that we have is to develop ourselves into becoming good people, "טובים" (people who have good מדות), and the *Mitzvos* are not merely isolated rules and guidelines, rather they are part of a self-development process.

The goal of the *mitzvos* is to help us to develop properly. In order for us to have good מדות, *Hashem* set up a system of מצות that are designed to help us develop good מדות. The development that *Hashem* is interested in is to have our thoughts and our hearts pure. Therefore, the *Torah* creates a system of *mitzvos* that are designed to help us to purify our thoughts and our hearts.

The ספר החינוך explains that many of the *mitzvos* are actions that we must do. The purpose of doing so many actions is because our thoughts and our hearts are influenced by our actions. This is an example of how *Hashem* designed the *mitzvos* with great wisdom and a clear understanding of human nature to help us develop properly.

אור הצפון - צלם אלוקים

A person was created "בצלם אלוקים", which refers to the fact that our nature is to act in the same ways that *Hashem* acts. "מה הוא רחום אף אתה רחום" is not merely a *mitzva*, rather, it is telling us that our responsibility is to use our *neshama*, which has a nature to act like *Hashem*, and we must actualize that greatness. We must develop ourselves in a way that enables our nature to come to the surface, and we must also act in this manner of emulating *Hashem*. The *mitzvos* that relate to this concept help us bring out our inborn greatness!

These are some of the examples of how *Hashem* created a תורה with the intention of helping a person to succeed in developing himself (to develop his מדות and to come close to *Hashem* and the תורה was designed to address a person's specific nature (as a human being) and to guide a person toward "Developing himself" within the reality of being a "human being" with all of the assets and challenges that his nature presents.

These examples demonstrate how much *Hashem* is interested in a person's success as we see that *Hashem* designed an intricate system to enable a person to succeed. However, we also see how much *Hashem* wanted to create a situation where it is very challenging for a person to succeed. Only through following the *Torah* properly, a person will be able to succeed because the specific system that a person requires is specifically created in a way that through keeping the *Torah* properly a person will be able to achieve his goals.

CHAPTER 24 - HOW DO WE USE THE MITZVOS TO DEVELOP OURSELVES?

Hashem understands the exact design of a human. With that understanding Hashem designed the Torah and the Mitzvos in order to help a person develop properly.

After we ask ourselves, "What is the purpose of my life?" we must ask ourselves, "How do I fulfill that purpose?" And if we are taking the purpose of our lives as our ultimate task in life, we must then ask ourselves, "How can I fulfill that purpose to the greatest extent possible?" This leads to the following inquiry- How do I work? How do I use my nature and my design to serve Hashem properly? Can I develop myself in a way that will enable me to serve Hashem better? How?"

The understanding of our nature, our design, and the way we work is obviously crucial, but it is also extremely complicated. To use our nature and our design to serve Hashem properly, and to develop ourselves into the best עבד ה' that we can be, we must understand ourselves thoroughly.

It would seem to be important and necessary for a person to have a clear understanding of the nature of a person's design, and to have a clear understanding of the nature of the mitzvos, and to understand how the mitzvos are helpful in a person's development; in order for a person to use the mitzvos productively to be able to develop himself properly.

The fact that the mitzvos are not merely about doing the actions, rather the goal is to develop our minds and our hearts properly, obviously makes our job more complicated. It requires much more of an understanding of human nature in order to know how to develop our minds and hearts properly. It also requires an understanding of how the *mitzvos* work in order to develop our minds and hearts properly.

It is also clear from the nature of many of the *mitzvos* that it is really challenging for a person to avoid being affected by his nature in a negative way. The *mitzvos* are designed to help a person protect himself, however if a person doesn't understand how to protect himself then it's not going to work.

However, in order for us to dedicate ourselves to understanding these areas, we need to recognize that it is important and necessary to understand these matters. If we think that we can just work hard to do the *mitzvos* and that alone will help us to develop his מדות properly then we will not be motivated to put the proper effort and focus into studying these matters.

CHAPTER 25 - WHY IS IT DIFFICULT FOR US TO RECOGNIZE THAT OUR DAILY LIVES HAVE MEANING AND VALUE?

It is common to find purpose, meaning, significance, and value when we are faced with an important opportunity or an important responsibility. However, we usually associate importance only with extreme behaviors or accomplishments. A standard act of kindness is generally not considered to be a major accomplishment, in order for it to rate, we must do something extreme, we must help in a significant way. We have to either feed many hungry people, or one person who is starving, we have to either save a sick person's life, or bring medicine to help many people feel better. We have to either solve someone's major business crisis, or create new jobs for a whole group of people. In those types of situations, we feel important and we feel like our lives have value and significance. However, if we help someone pay a few of his bills, or if we help him buy a few more groceries, or if we give someone advice for his business that helps him in a small way, it's hard to feel like we have accomplished anything significant.

Similarly, we can feel pride, significance, and value when we receive public praise. This could be because we have achieved something of significance, (in any one of a number of areas, sports, academics, or finances), or if there is something about us that seems to be significant, (we are strong, smart, beautiful, popular). This also usually requires something that is extreme in order to think about it as important. We generally view smaller, less extreme situations as being relatively meaningless.

Therefore, since most people, most of the time, have typical lives, and typical situations in life, they view themselves and most of their lives as relatively meaningless. Most of our lives are spent doing seemingly mundane activities. We all eat, sleep, work, and socialize. We take care of the basic needs of our families. Supper, bedtime, baths, homework, and carpool are a major part of our lives. We do find time for spirituality, we *daven*, *bentch*, make *brachos*, study *Torah*, and do *chessed*. However, most of us don't have the time or the means to do any of these in an extreme type of fashion.

This reality of the simplicity of our lives holds us back from being motivated to serve *Hashem* to our greatest capacity, and it holds us back from feeling good about the value of our lives, and the value of our accomplishments, and it holds us back from finding passion, meaning, purpose, and significance in our service of *Hashem*.

Hashem created the world for each of us and *Hashem* gave each of us an important mission.

The most basic part of recognizing our true purpose and our real value is the recognition that we have a purpose. This begins with the fact that *Hashem* created the world, and everything in the world was created by *Hashem* for a purpose. The next basic element is the recognition that we have an important purpose. This begins with the fact that *Hashem* created the entire world for the benefit of humans, and then we need to recognize that *Hashem* created the world for each person individually. A third factor that is also important is the fact that *Hashem* values each of the *mitzvos* in a very significant way. Therefore, any person who is involved with any of the *mitzvos* is doing something that is very important.

<u>אור הצפון - ספר תולדות האדם</u>
כל תכלית הבריאה כדי לקיים מצוה קלה אחת...כמה גדול ערכו של קיום מצוה אחת.. כדאי היה לברוא את כל העולם רק כדי שיקיים אדם אחד, מצוה אחת, ולשעה אחת. כל אדם ובכל הדורות ראוי הוא שבשביל מצוה אחת יבראו לו כל העולמות כולם...לכל יחיד ויחיד.

The *Alter* spells out that the same way that when *Hashem* created the world initially, He created it for *Adam* and *Hashem* gave him only one *mitzva*, because the world was worthwhile to have been created for one person and only for one *mitzva*. So too, the same is true for every person and for every *mitzva*. The *Alter* spells out that this is true nowadays also, even though we are not nearly on the same level as they used to be, however, it is still true that *Hashem* values us and our actions.

Am I Really So Important? What is so important about my life?

The fact that *Hashem* created us in *Hashem's* image, and the fact that the entire world was created for the purpose of each of us individually, tells us that each of our lives are extremely significant. However, it is difficult to believe that our lives are really important and significant. It is difficult to understand what it means that we were created in the image of *Hashem*, and it is certainly difficult to relate to.

The greatness of man is so far away from our understanding that there are people who have a hard time understanding why we prioritize human needs over animal needs. It's also difficult to understand what is so important about what we are doing and accomplishing in our lives? What are we doing that is so important that *Hashem* would create an entire world for us? If we were doing good things with extreme quality and quantity; either we did *chessed* all day and we cared about people with all of our hearts, or, if we *davened* to *Hashem* with the greatest amount of gratitude and humility, or, if we studied *Torah* for eighteen hours a day. Then we may understand why *Hashem* would create the world for us.

However, that's not our reality, and therefore, it's often hard to really believe that our lives are so important, and it's hard to know where to focus our energy if we want to try hard to serve *Hashem* with passion and dedication.

The *Mesilas Yesharim* teaches us that this drive for excellence in *Avodas Hashem*, without the clarity about where to channel the drive, often leads to misdirected thoughts, feelings, and actions. It causes people to do extreme behaviors, which are not really productive. Therefore, it's important to figure out what our important mission really is, and where to direct our passion and our dedication.

The *Alter* helps us understand the fact that people were created with a צלם אלוקים:

אור הצפון - צלם אלוקים
הליכה בדרכי השם..מתאימה היא..בדמותו וצלמו של האדם, כמחייבת את האדם שיהיה מה שהוא ראוי להיות באמת מראשית יצירתו, ולהוציא אל הפועל מה שיש לו בכח, להתדמות אל יוצרו.

In order to have an understanding of the fact that we are created בצלם אלוקים, we need to understand that the way we relate to *Hashem* is only through recognizing *Hashem's* attributes, which are the thirteen *middos* of *Hashem*. These *middos* relate to *chessed* and *emes*. This helps us realize that true greatness and accomplishment is achieved through having these attributes and acting with them.

Therefore, human greatness is also related to our *neshama*, which has in its nature to desire to act with *chessed* and *emes*. When we are developing these *middos* and we are acting based on them, we are accomplishing the ultimate in greatness. However, often the true value of *chessed* and *emes* is not appreciated, and therefore, our ability to act with these *middos* doesn't translate in our minds to greatness, and therefore, we are left wondering whether there really is true human greatness in the average person.

There are a few important concepts that explain what makes our everyday lives, which seem to be mundane and relatively unimportant, to be very significant, important, and full of tremendous spiritual achievement:

- We are all created צלם אלוקים, in the image of *Hashem*, and everything that we do is an act that is being performed by a צלם אלוקים, whether it's an act of הכרת הטוב by a צלם אלוקים, or an act of חסד or אמת that's performed by a צלם אלוקים etc. That perspective gives us an ability to appreciate a standard act that we perform in a much more significant way.

- The fact that we are serving *Hashem* alone is such an important matter, regardless of which *mitzvos* that we are doing or how many *mitzvos* that we are doing, it is such an important matter. *Hashem* told *Yeshaya Hanavi* that if he has a true appreciation of the value of being a עבד השם then he would be happy with his accomplishments in life, because the ability to serve *Hashem* is a very special honor (ישיעה-פרק מט'-רד"ק שם על מה שאמר השם לישעיה-הנקל בעיניך להיות עבד השם).

- Every time that we are doing a *mitzva*, we are demonstrating that we know that *Hashem* created the world, that *Hashem* runs the world, that *Hashem* gave us an amazing world with amazing opportunities for eternal happiness and that we would like to show our gratitude to *Hashem* by doing *Hashem's mitzvos*. (רמב"ן סוף פרשת בא).

- It's also extremely important to understand the value of matters such as חסד, אמת etc. The more that we appreciate that every seemingly simple act of kindness or honesty, is so important, then the more that we can understand how in regular everyday life we can accomplish so much.

- The fact that *Hashem* values effort and not tangible results is often helpful for us to focus on because it can help us to appreciate that our efforts are valuable even if we are not given the opportunity for tangible accomplishments.

- The fact that *Hashem* knows what our challenges are, is helpful to reassure us that *Hashem* has realistic expectations of us, and He doesn't expect perfection, and *Hashem* also values how much that we had to overcome in order to be able to have done as much as we did.

- It's also helpful to realize that *Hashem* created each of us with a different nature, and *Hashem* gives us a different set of experiences, and therefore, our job and our mission is individualized and unique. Therefore, we shouldn't measure our success based on how we compare to others, because our jobs are different, and our expectation is different.

- Our true purpose in the world is to develop our *neshama* properly. The actions that we do are important, but their purpose is not because there are things that need to be accomplished and we need to fix *Hashem's* world for Him. Rather, our actions are merely a means that *Hashem* created for us in order to develop our *neshamas*. When we recognize this, then we won't measure our success based on how big that our external accomplishments are, rather, we will focus on whether we are developing our sincerity and our *middos* as much as we can.

- Related to this is the focus that it's an important accomplishment to develop the proper thoughts and perspectives, not only is it objectively an important accomplishment, it's also helpful because even if we are not going to be able to change our behaviors so much, we still can grow internally.

The World Tells Us That Extreme and Tangible Accomplishments Are Important

Our perspectives are often shaped from the messages that we have received from the world from the time that we were young. We have generally heard that success should be defined based upon extreme and tangible accomplishments. We receive these messages in many different ways.

אור הצפון - חסד התורה

חוב על האדם לנער את האבק העבה שנצבר עליו זה כמה ממצביו השונים,
ומחשפעת חיי חפשטות וחגסוס של חסביבה אשר חי בתוכח. עבודח רבח
היא..לפעמים גם ירושה של הרבה דורות....אינו מוציא את עצמו ראוי לטובה
כזו, כי עוד לא התרומם ממצב פשטותו..

The way that we think about ourselves is based upon the way that we have been taught to think about ourselves. We receive many messages from the world around us about how important that we really are. Some of these messages are clearly stated and some are understood from the context of our words. Many of the messages are not even communicated verbally. When someone who is considered to be important enters a room, he is treated in a manner of importance. Everyone gives him attention, and everyone looks for him to receive attention from him. If he needs something, everyone views it as an honor to help him with his needs. However, when the average person walks into the room, nobody really cares too much. People generally view it as an annoyance to be busy with taking care of their needs. When someone does something that seems to be an extreme accomplishment, then he receives a message of importance and significance. However, when we go through the average day, even when we are involved in good things, we do not receive messages of importance. We are receiving a clear message about who is really important and about what is really important in life.

These messages begin when we are very young, we start to receive messages of who is important and what is important. These messages come from all of our interactions in life. They are clear and consistent messages that we receive for many, many years. These messages become the way that we understand the world and what is important in the world. The messages become so much part of our thinking that it is difficult to process it in any other fashion. Even if we would be taught to view things differently, it would be difficult to really believe it.

34584119R00051

Made in the USA
Middletown, DE
27 January 2019